PERGAMON INTERNATIONAL LIBRARY
of Science, Technology, Engineering and Social Studies

*The 1000-volume original paperback library in aid of education,
industrial training and the enjoyment of leisure*

Publisher: Robert Maxwell, M.C.

The Human Subject in the Psychological Laboratory

PGPS-68

W9-CKJ-384

PERGAMON GENERAL PSYCHOLOGY SERIES

Editor: Arnold P. Goldstein, *Syracuse University*
Leonard Krasner, *SUNY, Stony Brook*

The terms of our inspection copy service apply to all the above books. A complete catalogue of all books in the Pergamon International Library is available on request.

The Publisher will be pleased to receive suggestions for revised editions and new titles.

THE HUMAN SUBJECT
in the PSYCHOLOGICAL LABORATORY

Irwin Silverman

York University
Ontario, Canada

PERGAMON PRESS
New York / Toronto / Oxford / Sydney / Frankfurt / Paris

Pergamon Press Offices:

U.S.A.   Pergamon Press Inc., Maxwell House, Fairview Park,
                  Elmsford, New York 10523, U.S.A.

U.K.   Pergamon Press Ltd., Headington Hill Hall, Oxford OX3,
                  OBW, England

CANADA   Pergamon of Canada, Ltd., 207 Queen's Quay West,
                  Toronto 1, Canada

AUSTRALIA   Pergamon Press (Aust) Pty. Ltd., 19a Boundary Street,
                  Rushcutters Bay, N.S.W. 2011, Australia

FRANCE   Pergamon Press SARL, 24 rue des Ecoles,
                  75240 Paris, Cedex 05, France

WEST GERMANY   Pergamon Press GmbH, 6242 Kronberg/Taunus,
                  Frankfurt-am-Main, West Germany

Library of Congress Cataloging in Publication Data

Silverman, Irwin.
   The human subject in the psychological laboratory.

(Pergamon general psychology series : 68)
1. Human experimentation in psychology. I. Title

BF200.S49   150'.7'24   76-14815
ISBN 0-08-021080-5
ISBN 0-08-021079-1 pbk.

Printed in the United States of America

To my children, Amy and Laura

Contents

We have not succeeded in answering all our problems. Indeed, we sometimes feel we have not completely answered any of them. The answers we have found only serve to raise a whole set of new questions. In some ways we feel that we are as confused as ever, but we believe we are confused on a much higher plane and about more important questions.

(This quote was given me by Wilse B. Webb, who had carried it on his person for many years but didn't remember where he had found it.)

Preface

This book is about mystery, intrigue and deception. It does not deal with the doings of spies; it is about psychological experiments, but there are notable parallels. Spies contrive schemes, veiled in mystery, intrigue and deception, to extract hidden information from people, and so do psychologists. Further, the targets of spies, if they become aware that they are such, generally respond by providing false and misleading information, and so do psychological subjects.

The thesis of this book is that the psychological laboratory is a very special place for the people we bring there as subjects and, accordingly, they act in very special ways; ways that bear little relationship to their behaviors in the life situations to which we seek to generalize our findings. Chapters 1 and 2 are, mainly, an analysis of the motives, feelings and intentions that are common to people who assume the role of Psychological Subject. Chapters 3 through 5 describe and illustrate, from diverse areas of psychology, the ways in which subjects' role-related responses confound data and lead to spurious conclusions. The final chapter offers directions, as far as this author can envision them, toward a veridical psychology. The book was written for anyone who does or plans to do behavioral research.

As part of a graduate seminar, students read and wrote reviews of the manuscript, and one issue was raised with sufficient frequency that I feel it should be dealt with here. Throughout the book I have presented the findings of laboratory research designed to demonstrate the artifactual nature of other laboratory research. The question is: How can I conclude that data from psychological laboratories are almost inevitably confounded by role-related subject behavior and nevertheless accept the validity of the studies which purport to demonstrate this. I have two responses. The first, which is glib, is that if the reader is prompted to question the validity of the studies invoked as evidence for the arguments, on the basis of the arguments themselves, then the point has been made. The second, which more directly confronts the question, is that the laboratory is undoubtedly an excellent place to study laboratory behavior; the idiosyncratic motives and responses that are elicited in someone who takes the role of psychological subject, but *by virtue of this, it is suited for little else.*

Most of my own studies described herein were sponsored by grants from the National Science Foundation. During the years when they were my students and afterward, Arthur Shulman and David Wiesenthal shared with me many ideas on the topics of this book. I would like to express my debt, as well, to those who read sections of earlier drafts and added their encouragement and counsel: David Bakan, Arnold Goldstein, Sidney Jourard, Lucille Palmiere and J. Philippe Rushton, and to Leona Harrison for her help in the preparation of the manuscript and in guiding me to a better word or phrase when I needed it.

A special note of gratitude is due Sidney Jourard, whose untimely death was a profound loss to our field as well as to those of us who were privileged to know him. I have drawn liberally from his writings in these pages and often, when we were colleagues at the University of Florida, I sought and received his wisdom.

1

Psychological Subject as a Role

ECOLOGY OF THE PSYCHOLOGICAL EXPERIMENT

The method of choice of the research psychologist is the experiment. He has created his discipline beside his forebears in ethology, anthropology, and sociology by forsaking, to a great extent, description of natural occurring events in favor of manipulation and control.

Psychological experiments can conceivably be performed in any number of settings, but, for functional reasons, they usually occur in a very specialized space—a room or two in a university or other institution, probably with a marker reading *Psychological Laboratory* or something similar. Often a classroom is transformed into a laboratory for an hour or so, with the instructor making an announcement such as: "Today you are being asked to take part in a psychological experiment." Occasionally, the limits of the laboratory are expanded. In one instance (Newcomb, 1961), a college dormitory was created for research on the "acquaintance process" with residents living there without charge in return for their cooperation.

Though locations do vary, they have one consistent aspect: *They are the habitat, in a phenomenological sense, of the experimenter and not the subject.* Psychologists bring people to experiments rather than experiments to people. Our manipulanda and measurements are not focused on normal life routines; rather, they constitute an exotic interruption of these.

The advantages of conducting research in the experimenter's habitat are apparent. It affords a level of precision not readily attainable in the complex habitats of our human subjects. The question is, however: What is it that we are being so precise about? An animal in his own habitat and the same animal in a habitat contrived by people behaves quite differently, and ethologists are well aware of the pitfalls of trying to generalize from one situation to the other (Morris, 1968). We should expect humans, as well, to show atypical behavior in an atypical environment.

Simply stated, people feel and think, and people who are subjects in psychological experiments are undoubtedly feeling and thinking *about* the experiment. They may be feeling fear about looking foolish or incapable of revealing something about themselves which should best be kept secret. They may be feeling anger about being in such a situation, or awe, or wariness, or curiosity, or skepticism, or utter delight at being the focus of an important person's attention. They may be wondering what the meaning of their responses are to the experimenter; what sort of responses he expects; whether he is divulging the true purposes of his experiment to them. Whatever the nature of these thoughts and emotions, they are most likely quite consuming, for to be a subject in a psychological experiment must be more than a run-of-the-mill event, at least for the uninitiated. The seers and prophets of earlier days have given way to Behavioral Scientists, and one does not stand easy before their scrutiny.

To the extent that the subject's feelings and thoughts about the experiment are prepotent, they will inevitably interact with the experimental manipulations and contribute to his responses. Considering the ingenuity that is often used to try to conceal manipulations from subjects, it seems that researchers are at least implicitly aware of this, but subjects need not be cognizant of the experimenter's hypothesis for the effect of the situation to be present. For example, in a frequently quoted study, Hovland and Weiss (1951) showed that subjects were persuaded more than three times as much by arguments attributed to a high credible source than by the same arguments attributed to a low credible source. But should we expect other than this from people who are performing in the super-intellectual climate of a behavioral science laboratory under the watchful eye of a professorial-type experimenter? Do these findings tell us anything about the person's attention to the sources of arguments heard at a political rally or read, in private, in a newspaper editorial?

The psychological experiment does indeed inspire some very unusual behaviors on the part of the people who perform in them. Orne (1962) reports that most subjects, when simply asked to, will do serial addition tasks on random numbers for several hours with little decrement in performance or show of hostility, and that they persist as long and as cheerfully when they are instructed to *destroy each worksheet as they complete it.* This is not difficult to understand in a setting in which the person has accepted the servile label of "subject" with all of its connotations, but we would be hard pressed to find another situation in which people show such mindless, passive subservience. Yet this is the place in which we study such states as frustration, conformity, aggression, dependency, etc., with the untroubled assumption that the behaviors we observe are representative of what our subjects do in their real worlds.

Milgram (1963), in fact, considered the experimenter-subject relationship to be uniquely appropriate for the study of extreme cases of "destructive obedience." Subjects were instructed to administer increasing levels of electric shock to a person alleged to be another subject (he was actually the experimenter's confederate, and the shock was hoked) as part of a so-called punishment-learning study. Subjects were convinced, according to their later reports, of the authenticity of the study and most showed signs of marked psychological discomfort (trembling, sweating, bizarre laughing). Twenty-six of 40, however, continued to the maximum level of 450 volts when the experimenter requested them to, even though the actor-confederate had stopped responding and was heard pounding the wall of the room in which he was allegedly bound to the shock apparatus.

It is emphasized that Milgram did not consider these findings indicative of people's general propensities for either cruelty or compliance. Rather, he described in some detail the features of the psychological experiment which rendered it possible to induce this unusual behavior: The unimpeachable image of the university which was the "background authority of the study," the lofty ideals associated with psychological experimentation, the sense of obligation felt by the subject to the experimenter, and the subject's vagueness about what constituted appropriate behavior in this situation in his role as such. These same persons would probably refuse to continue if asked by an employer or teacher or parent, but in those settings they would be in quite different roles.

The venerable concept of *role* provides an apt framework for understanding the behavior of subjects. In its broadest definition, a role refers to *all of the cognitive and affective states of an individual related to his perception of his position in a given interpersonal situation.* People occupy many roles in the course of a day, which often call for divergent and contradictory behaviors, and to understand any bit of interpersonal behavior we usually need to be aware of the person's role at the time. Consider a loan officer of a bank talking to someone without collateral. The attributes of selflessness, altruism, generosity, and sympathy would hardly apply to him, but if we watch the same person interacting with his family we would probably emerge with quite a different concept.

The psychological experiment is, after all, an interpersonal interaction between subject and experimenter, and the subject's behavior can no more be isolated from his role than the banker's from the position he occupies. Further, the generalizability of our observations from laboratory to life will suffer the same short-comings as an attempt to construct generalities about the banker's altruism or generosity at home from his behavior at his job.

HISTORICAL AND CONTEMPORARY USES OF SUBJECTS: THE CYCLE OF INTROSPECTIONSIM

At the beginnings of human psychological experimentation, there was less ambiguity associated with the role of subject than exists today. Subjects of the "structuralism-introspectionist" era (dating from the establishment of Wundt's laboratory in 1879) were full collaborators in the execution of research, highly trained in the art of observing and reporting their own conscious experience. The psychologist was often both experimenter and subject and, when not, the subject was usually his graduate student.

Nevertheless, there was considerable thought to role-related behavior as a source of interference, for the investigator carefully screened his subject-observers to exclude those whom he believed incapable of objective introspection. Titchener (1912) stipulated that the introspectionist-subject must be free from anxiety and comfort-able in the experimental surroundings and, as Schultz (1969) points out, as many as 70 percent of Titchener's subjects were eliminated from a single study when they were "found to be incapable of reacting with any degree of constancy" (Titchener, 1895, p. 75).

The demise of introspectionism began with the functional

schools of the early 1900's and, for all purposes, was completed with the advent of Watsonian behaviorism in the second decade. Then the concept of subject underwent a marked transition from "collabo-rator-observer" to "object." From that point, psychological experimentation required that the subject be untrained and uninformed about the investigator's intentions. Rather than an observer or "reagent" (a substance used to detect and examine other substances), as he was often called by the structuralists, he was regarded as a passive entity which received experimental manipulanda and gave off measurable responses. Psychologists came to regard putting input into a human subject as something akin to putting chemicals into a test tube, and are just slowly realizing that it is inevitably an unclean test tube, contaminated by all of the subjective states and dispositions of someone who knows that his behavior is being scrutinized as part of a psychological experiment. No one told the *subject* to stop introspecting and, even if he were told, it is unlikely that he could.

History has a way of reappearing, and, as we come to this understanding, there is a faint, but unmistakable call for a return of sorts to introspectionist methods. Three current views in this vein, expressed by psychologists well known in their areas, are presented below:

In a recent paper, Fine (1969) said*

> ... it should be abundantly clear that psychological science cannot proceed by rejecting and ignoring introspection. It must rather accept introspection as a tool and subject it to the same kind of scientific investigation. It is a phenomenon to be studied, subject to the same kind of scientific controls that other tools and phenomena are subjected to. (p. 521)

According to Fine, in the "fundamental formula, $R = f(O,S)$, where R is the response, O is the organism and S is the stimulus . . . it is clear that in the determination of some responses the organism may play a more important role or the stimulus may play a more important role" (p. 528). The methods of contemporary psychology, he continues, are conducive to "stimulus bound" responses, which are often inappropriate for the construct under investigation. In studies of aesthetic preferences, for example,

*Reprinted with permission of author and publisher from: Fine, Reuben. On the nature of scientific method in psychology. *PSYCHOLOGICAL REPORTS*, 1969, 24, 519-540.

S is asked whether he likes or dislikes certain forms or shapes, or asked to compare two shapes and tell which one he likes more or less. He sooner or later drifts into those aspects of the situation which are determined by the form, that is, judgments, and stays away from those aspects of the situation which are determined by his inner feelings. . . . If we had to investigate why one picture in a gallery is pleasing to one person, while displeasing to another, the problem could not adequately be tackled merely by an experimental approach; we would have to resort to introspective observations and careful investigation of each individual. (p. 529)

Jourard (1969) regards psychological research with humans as "a special case of research in self disclosure." He states:*

The claim holds true whether we are investigating factors in subjects' willingness to reveal personal information about themselves through interviews, or factors affecting the learning of nonsense syllables, operant rates, eyelid conditioning, perception, recall—the whole range of topics which psychologists study. When we ask a person to report what he sees on a screen, remember something, or let us watch him as he masters a list of words, he is disclosing something about himself to an audience. (p. 110)

The problem, according to Jourard, is that the model of psychological experimentation in which the procedures and intents of the study are shrouded in secrecy, subjects are deceived and depersonalized, and the researcher takes the role of a "white-coated, anonymous, impersonal eminence," is totally nonconducive to self-disclosure of any sort. "Man certainly does live much of his life in relation to high status anonymous strangers, before whom he conceals most of his experience; his behavior under usual laboratory conditions is perhaps generalizeable to that aspect of his life" (p. 111).

Jourard suggests a new "humanistic" model for psychological research, based on a concept of the experiment as an interpersonal

*This and other quotations below (unless otherwise noted) of the late Dr. Jourard are from Jourard, S.M. The effects of experimenter's self-disclosure on subjects' behavior. In C.N. Spielberger (Ed.) *Current Topics in Clinical and Community Psychology.* New York: Academic Press, 1969. Pp. 109-150.

interaction in which experimenter and subject collaborate in the search for information, much like the role ascribed to subject in the introspectionist times. Studies may be conducted, he says, "by the subject himself. Let him, like Ebbingaus sitting in his attic learning lists of nonsense syllables, serve as both experimenter and subject, making use of all gadgetry available to record his behavior and experience" (p. 112).

A similar view is expounded by Kelman (1967), who expresses his displeasure with traditional experimental procedures and advocates a new approach which will "involve the subject as an active participant in a joint effort with the experimenter."

Specifically, Kelman feels that rather than the widespread use of deception in the induction of experimental variables, we substitute "some sort of role-playing" of the research problem on the part of the subject; he suggests, for example, that we inform people about deceptions in the experimental design before they enter the experiment and ask them "to react as if they really found themselves in this situation."

Whether or not we accept neo-introspectionism in any of these forms as a solution, the concerns of Fine and Jourard and Kelman typify the disenchantment of many with the concept of subject as object underlying most contemporary research.

SOURCES OF PSYCHOLOGICAL SUBJECTS

With the transition in the concept of subject from self-observer to object, there was no longer a need to limit samples to the select population of psychologists and psychology trainees able and motivated to do "introspective work." In fact, with the emphasis on individual differences stemming from the functionalist school and with the excursion of psychology into behaviors with more complex experiential bases, valid generalizations required more heterogeneous subject samples.

At the onset of the post-structuralist era, psychologists turned to the most readily available source of supply: the undergraduate. In the ensuing 60 years, however, they have turned no further, and subject samples are, if anything, more restricted and homogeneous now than they were in Titchener's time.

McNemar, in 1946, complained that, "The existing science of human behavior is largely the science of the behavior of sophomores" (p. 333). Three surveys, reported 20 to 25 years later, provided empirical support.

Smart (1966) recorded the sources of subjects (excluding psychiatric samples) from the two largest journals of the American Psychological Association containing primarily human research: *The Journal of Abnormal and Social Psychology* for the years 1962-1964 and the *Journal of Experimental Psychology* for 1963-1964. Schultz (1969) performed the same analyses on the same journals for 1966-1967, (using the *Journal of Personality and Social Psychology* which was one of the two journals created by the split of *Journal of Abnormal and Social Psychology*).

Jung (1969) used a somewhat different approach, with the advantage that he did not have to interpret the often ambiguous descriptions of subject samples in the journals. He circulated a questionnaire about subject recruitment to the 60 graduate departments of psychology generating the largest numbers of doctorates, to which 52 responded.

The findings of the three surveys are summarized in Table 1.

Table 1. Sources of human subjects according to three surveys

Subject sources	Smart (1966)		Schultz (1969)		Jung (1969)
	JASP[a]	JEP[b]	JPSP[c]	JEP[d]	
Introductory psychology	32%	42%	34%	41%	80%
Other college	41%	44%	36%	43%	11%
Non-college	27%	14%	30%	13%	10%

[a]*Journal of Abnormal and Social Psychology*

[b]*Journal of Experimental Psychology*

[c]*Journal of Personality and Social Psychology*

[d]In 3.5 percent of the articles in this group the sources of subjects were not reported.

Both Smart's and Schultz's studies show that about 70 percent of subjects in social psychological and personality research, and about 85 percent in the areas served by *Journal of Experimental Psychology* (learning, perception, cognition, etc.) are college students, with about half of these from the introductory psychology course. Despite the three-year interim, there is a remarkable correspondence between findings, suggesting that, for better or worse, subject sampling procedures are very stable.

Jung's data agree in general with the other two in terms of percentages of college students (91 percent), but he finds that *80 percent are from the introductory psychology course.* Most likely, Jung's figures are the more accurate: journal articles often describe subject samples simply as "college students," whereas many of these are probably from the introductory course.

On the other hand, Smart and Schultz surveyed published studies while Jung included all research, published or otherwise. Thus, the discrepancy may be based, in part, on the interesting possibility that experiments using college subjects other than introductory students have a higher probability of being successful and appearing in the literature. These subjects are more likely to be volunteers (Jung notes that introductory courses most always have a requirement for participation) and, if they are upperclassmen and have been in the introductory course previously, they have more experience as subjects (Jung finds that of the 11 percent of college subjects who are not from the introductory course, about four-fifths are from advanced psychology courses). There are findings, to be discussed in more detail in later chapters, suggesting that both of these factors increase the likelihood that the subjects' role-behaviors will help to confirm the experimental hypothesis.

In any case, it is clear that a vast majority of subjects are drawn from the college student population, with most of these from introductory psychology and the bulk of the remainder from other psychology courses.

The stereotype of the subject does not end here, for not only do they come from the same place, they are obtained in much the same manner. According to Jung's survey, 92 percent of college students are coerced by means of some reward or threat of punishment related to course grades. Forty-five percent are recruited by a blanket course requirement; for 25 percent there is a requirement but with an alternative of additional course work of some sort; 22 percent are offered extra credits toward their grade for participation.

How are these coercions justified to students? Jung finds that in 97 percent of cases they are told by the department that subject participation is part of their education in psychology. In 64 percent of these cases, the rationale includes some statements about the needs of researchers.

How frequently do the same subjects tend to serve? According to

Jung, the mean number of sessions demanded by departments with a requirement or option is four, and for some schools it is as many as eight or ten. We might assume that the small proportion of volunteer subjects also includes many repeaters, people interested in the experience or the monetary gain (Jung reports that of the 7 percent of volunteer subjects, about two-fifths are paid).

The issue of the generalizability of findings from college students to the population at large, assuming that subjects do respond in experiments in ways that are veridical to their naturalistic behavior, is well considered by Smart, Schultz, and Jung. Beyond that issue, however, is the question of what special characteristics there are in an undergraduate psychology student subject, recruited as part of a course requirement or option, which contribute to his feelings and percepts about the experiment.

First, the psychology student subject has, undoubtedly, more than passing interest in the field and the experiment being conducted and, unless he is drawn at the very beginning of his introductory course, he has some degree of sophistication about psychological research methods. Thus, he is far from being a passive object; in fact, he is probably very much engrossed in what we are trying to find out about him.

Further, the experimenter he serves is also a professor or professor-delegate in the institution where he is a student, who has considerable status and power in relation to him. This will probably add to the subject's concern about what he shows about himself.

He is, in addition, performing an option or requirement that he is told is part of his education. If he does not believe this, it may make him belligerent; if he does, it is logical to assume this will increase his attention to the experimental procedures and the meanings of his responses to them.

Finally, he is more likely than not a veteran subject, who brings to the experiment the effects of whatever manipulations, surprises, or deceptions he has encountered beforehand.

The ways by which all of these factors may increase the potential confounding of experimental observations by subject role-behavior will be considered in detail in later chapters. For now, we will make the apparent conclusion that there are some very special attributes of the subject-experimenter relationship inherent in the sterotypic samples and sampling procedures psychologists use.

ROLE BEHAVIOR OF SUBJECTS: EARLY CONTRIBUTIONS

The notions we have introduced here are not new to psychology, but they are newly respected. Prior to the early 1960's, considerations about the subject role were contained in what Friedman (1967) described as, "A folklore of offhand remarks and offbeat articles" (p. 26).

These date to Ebbingaus in 1885, who considered that, in both the roles of experimenter and subject, the expectancies he acquired from the early data of his studies, "constitute a complicating factor which probably has a definite influence upon the subsequent results" (p. 28).[1]

Titchener (1901) cautioned also about the sensitivity of subjects to cues by the experimenter regarding his hypothesis. "Introspection," he said, "becomes doubly difficult when one knows the E desires one to reach a predetermined result. Many experimental series have been spoiled by some suggestion by E and an answering complaisanse on the part of O" (p. xiii).

In 1914, Fernberger surmised that in psychophysical studies, despite instructions to judge a stimuli as less than, more than, or equal to another in some quality, subjects tended not to give equality judgments. This, he reasoned, was because the subject desires to "do well" and believes "that the giving of equality judgments is an indication that he cannot discriminate so accurately" (p. 542). Fernberger found that by altering standard instructions to assure the subject that equality judgments were often appropriate, the proportion of these was significantly increased. He concluded that "one can only say that a given sensitivity has been found to exist *under certain given experimental conditions.* Inasmuch as we are dealing with a total psychophysical organism, and not merely with a sense organ, it is, after all, not surprising that the attitude of the subject should have a profound effect upon this sensitivity" (p. 542).

Stumberg, in 1925, reported data to the effect that subjects who were knowledgeable about the word-association method of detecting areas of conflict could successfully prevent detection. She cautioned

[1] More than 75 years later Rosenthal and his students (Rosenthal, Persinger, Vikan-Kline, & Fode, 1963) undertook a study requiring subjects to judge dispositions from photographs in which the first two subjects (actually confederates) seen by each experimenter supplied data which either confirmed or disconfirmed the experimental hypothesis. The judgments obtained by these two groups of experimenters from their subsequent subjects were significantly different, in the direction of the expectations that had been implanted in them.

about artifact in general based on psychological sophistication of subjects.

In 1930, articles by both Anderson and Wells attempted to delineate and describe the consequences of different attitudes of subjects toward experimental tasks. Anderson stated:*

> ... the experimenter cannot safely assume that his O's [observers] actually adopt and constantly maintain the experimental posture which is called for in the formal instruction. In the first place, certain *self* instructions inevitably color the performance (e.g., "I am easily distracted in this sort of experiment," "I *must* find a difference between these sounds"). And again, the occasion or setting itself always instructs ("That 's' [stimulus] obviously calls for transposition." "The light went off too suddenly."). That is *occasional* instruction. It is very insidious and powerful. It may have a greater effect upon the functional outcome than the formal instruction itself. (p. 345)

Both authors spoke of the pervasive self-consciousness of the "laboratory attitude." According to Anderson:

> The observer here is on the alert in surveying or critically scrutinizing himself as an observer in the experiment. He wants assurance that he is "properly set" or is "ready to observe" or that he is following out the command contained in the formal instruction. He feels his responsibility as an observer to carry out to the best of his ability the task which has been set him. This attitude breaks in upon the course of the experience which is bound up with the experimental stimulation, and it temporarily blocks that course. (p. 352)

Wells considered that: "The common-sense attitude is the attitude with which we meet affective experience in everyday life outside of the laboratory, as opposed to the attitude of psychological observation in an experimental situation. It is a 'natural' unrestricted set, a set to react naively to whatever comes without attempting to scrutinize experience" (p. 575).

Rosenzweig, in 1933, provided the most extensive and, in terms

*Reprinted by permission.

of current concerns of psychologists, far-sighted of the early papers on subject role-behavior, titled "The experimental situation as a psychological problem." He contended that:

> ... when one works with human materials one must reckon with the fact that everyone is a psychologist. How many subjects in a psychological experiment are purely receptive? How many are willing fully to adopt the humble role of subject in an investigation of their motives, aims and thoughts? Most, as a matter of fact, are carrying on a train of psychological activity that is rather about the experiment than a part of it by the intention of the Er (experimenter). . . . Moreover, *the Ee* [subject or observer] *is himself often unaware of the insidious ways in which these extraneous motivational factors have crept into and influenced the experiment.* (p. 342)

Rosenzweig spoke of "pride" and "compliance" as the two major facets of the subject's extraneous motivation. The confounding of experimental observations by pride is illustrated by the "Ee who says he has liked better certain puzzles on which he has failed than certain others on which he has succeeded." (This is a reference, one assumes, to the classic "Zeignarnik" effect which the Gestalt psychologists attributed to the need for closure.) "Interrogation soon shows that he reports this because, in his opinion, only a weak character would prefer easy to hard things. He is therefore telling the Er not what he did like but what he thinks he ought to have liked" (p. 344).

When compliance is the dominant motive, on the other hand, the subject aims "not to preserve his own respect but to save the Ers" (p. 345) by conforming in his responses to whatever he perceives is the experimental hypothesis. Occasionally, Rosenzweig noted, subjects will be "negatively suggestible," which "makes itself manifest in a desire to influence the experiment to the dissatisfaction of the Er" (p. 345).

He spoke also of the effects of the "total given personality" of the experimenter upon the subject:

> Whether the Er is, for instance, a man or woman, white or black, Jewish or Gentile, are factors that might make a difference to the attitude and reactions of the Ee. There are even changes in the personality of the same Er from hour to

hour or day to day that may alter the experimental condition to which different Ee's are subject. Whenever factors of this type *have been uncontrolled* and have played a part in an experiment, 'errors of personality influence' may be said to have occurred. To obviate such errors it is helpful if the experiment can be designed so as to proceed without the Er's presence, but when this is not possible, the systematic variation of Er's with comparable groups of Ee's is a useful expedient. (pp. 351-352)

Rosenzweig described further the concept of "suggestion error," whereby the experimenter subtly and inadvertently communicates his expectancies for the subject's responses to him. "It is not difficult to see how an unguarded word, nod, or glance from the Er may have a suggestive significance of marked consequence to certain experimental results" (p. 352).

It is noteworthy that Rosenzweig's contributions were relegated to the psychological archives in almost complete obscurity. For about 25 years following, even the folklore about extraneous subject behavior was thin, with the exception, perhaps, of Brunswick's (1947) classic paper on the need for representation of experimenters in psychological research. Then, in the late 1950's, there was a rumble of concern, highlighted by papers by Criswell (1958) and Riecken (1962). (Though Riecken's was published in 1962, it was first presented at the 1958 convention of the American Psychological Association.)

Criswell described the subject role as essentially one of "gaming" behavior, that is, solving the problem of what responses are appropriate for the experiment. She discussed (1958),* as one illustration, a much-cited study of small group dynamics by Festinger and Thibaut (1951):

> ... subjects are to discuss a certain problem by passing notes to each other. They have each received data of such a nature as to force their opinions far apart on a scale. Each keeps a card in front of him expressing the scale value of his opinion. After opinions are set, the subjects are told to discuss the problem by passing notes to each other. One outcome of the experiment is that more notes are passed to persons who

*Reprinted by permission.

deviate most from the modal opinion of the group. This result is interpreted as partially supporting a theory that groups tend toward a uniformity of state, exerting pressure toward uniformity on their members.

The experiment can be more simply interpreted by considering what action alternatives the subjects actually had. They were told to discuss a problem by passing notes. Theoretically the notes could contain any sort of conversation, but such possibilities were pretty well ruled out by the instructions to the subjects. They are to discuss something, and if they are good, cooperative subjects, this is what they will do. If you discuss something, what do you do? Statements of agreement would not produce much discussion. Here the experiment seems to illustrate subjects' willingness to play a game for the experimenter rather than a group's compelling movements toward uniformity. (pp. 105-6)

The lead sentence of Riecken's article reflects the feeling of discovery of contemporary psychologists about the extraneous motives of subjects: "The present paper is a first attempt to outline a problem in empirical social psychology and to suggest some ways of attacking it" (p. 25).

Riecken, as Criswell, stressed the problem-solving nature of the subject's behavior. He noted* that:

> The fact the experimenter controls the information available to the subject and that he never reveals completely what he is trying to discover and how he will judge what he observes— this feature gives the experiment much of its character as a game or contest. It leads to a set of inferential and interpretive activities on the part of the subject in an effort to penetrate the experimenter's inscrutability and to arrive at some conception of the meaning that the unrevealed categories of response have for the latter. (p. 31)

The subject tries to solve the riddle of the experiment, according to Riecken, because he wants "to represent himself as favorably as possible or to 'put his best foot forward' " (p. 34).

*Reprinted by permission.

The subject, therefore, must adopt a peculiar posture. He must be (or appear to be) cooperative in order to find out the meaning of his own actions as these are given meaning by the experimenter's interpretations. Yet he must have some basis for deciding how to act before he knows what his acts mean. He must make some approximation of the meaning of the situation in order to take a step that will yield some information that permits him to revise (or confirm) his first approximation. He must, necessarily, adopt a cut-and-dry or iterative procedure for solving his problem. (p. 34)

Riecken concludes that this "deutero-problem" of subjects, "plays some role in all experimental situations and for all subjects and may, on some occasions, be more important than the 'task' or 'treatment' in explaining results" (p. 34).

It was in this period also that attention became focused on sources of invalidity in many types of psychological tests, particularly measures of personality and opinions, based on subjects' tendencies to respond in "socially desirable" ways (Edwards, 1957).

In the early 1960's the rumble grew louder, heralded by the early writings of Orne (1962) on the "demand characteristics" of psychological research, defined as "the totality of cues which convey an experimental hypothesis to the subject" (p. 779), and Rosenthal (1963) on the ways by which experimenters covertly communicate such cues to subjects. In the last decade, probably no other topic occupied psychologists as extensively as "the social psychology of the psychological experiment." A survey (Shulman and Silverman, 1972) of the *Journal of Personality and Social Psychology* for the years 1965 through 1967 revealed that Orne (1962) was the single most frequently referenced article. Scarcely a general psychology convention passed without at least one symposium or paper session on the topic, and the literature seemed to amass at a progressively increasing rate.

THE WAITING OF THE ZEITGEIST

Considering this degree of current preoccupation, the hiatus of 25 years following Rosenzweig's (1933) paper seems particularly notable. Without exception, the notions he described are the same ones that compel our attention, under a brand new set of labels, today. "Compliance" is spoken of as conforming to "demand characteristics" (Orne, 1962); "negative suggestibility" is the "boomerang effect" (Silverman, 1965); "pride" goes by the title "evaluation apprehension" (Rosenberg, 1965); "errors of personality influence" are referred to as "experimenter effects" (Kintz et al., 1965); and "suggestion error" we know as "interpersonal expectations" (Rosenthal, 1969). The fact that the labels are generally more esoteric may or may not harbor significance regarding the progress of our discipline.

Thus, the concepts that should have been basic to the development of our research methods were not beyond our visibility or comprehension. Apparently, the *Zeitgeist* was lacking until the present, and historians may well ponder why.

A provocative article by Koch (1969) offers a hint. Koch takes a dim view* of the progress and prospects of psychology: "the massive 100 year effort to erect a discipline given to the positive study of man can hardly be counted a triumph. Here and there the effort has turned up a germane fact, or thrown off a spark of insight, but these victories have had an accidental relationship to the programs believed to have inspired them, and their sum total over time is heavily overbalanced by the pseudo-knowledge that has proliferated" (p. 14).

He attributes the failure of psychology to become a coherent science to the conditions of its beginnings.

> Prior to the late 19th Century, there are no precedents in the history of ideas for creating new fields of knowledge by edict. Sciences won their way to independence by achieving enough knowledge to become sciences. By the late 19th Century, these justly discriminated fields of science had given such food to man's cognitive and material hungers as to make his appetite insatiable. At the same time, inquiry into the nature and trend of science itself began to focus into an apparently wholesome Victorian vision: that of a totally ordered universe, totally open to the methods of science, and a totally ordered science, totally open to the strategems—and wants—of man. It was against this background that psychology was *stipulated* into life.

*From Koch, S. Psychology cannot be a coherent science. *Psychology Today*, 1969, 3, 14, 64-68. Copyright © 1969 Ziff-Davis Publishing Company. Reprinted by permission of *Psychology Today* Magazine.

At the time of its inception, psychology was unique in the extent to which its institutionalization preceded its content and its methods preceded its problem. . . .

For close to a century now, many psychologists have seemed to suppose that the methods of natural science are totally specifiable and specified; that the applicability of these methods to social and human events is not only an established fact but that no knowledge is worth taking seriously unless it is based on inquiries saturated with the iconology of science. Thus, from the very beginning, respectability held more glamor than insight, caution than curiosity, feasibility than fidelity. *The stipulation that psychology be adequate to science outweighed the commitment that it be adequate to man.* (p. 64, italics mine)

Whether or not we share Koch's pessimism, it seems feasible that many of psychology's mishaps stemmed from its historic compulsion to fit the study of behavior into extant models of other experimental sciences. Psychology was stipulated into life as an adolescent, but deprived of the critical formative stage of systematic naturalistic observation. Unique among the sciences, its hypotheses were traditionally conceived in the theoretician's armchair and carried directly to the experimentalist's laboratory. Naturalistic observation, as the initial enterprise of a science, not only points to heuristic questions for experimentation but suggests what methods and settings are and are not appropriate for such experiments.

But in their haste to reduce human behavior to the same microscopic proportions by which other sciences analyze the substances of their domains, psychologists could not afford the luxury of an indefinite period of just watching people do what they do. The result is that we have given selective inattention to the most important, but pithy facet of human psychological experimentation, the "ecological validity" (Brunswick, 1947) of our laboratory observations.

Researchers in other natural sciences confront the same type of problem. The biologist gives constant attention to the question of whether the conditions in his test tube (*in vitro*) are functionally the same as in the intact organism (*in vivo*). He deals, however, with something such as a blood sample and we deal with the behavior of a human being who is seduced or coerced to "take part in a psychological experiment," and the problem of the comparability of laboratory and life is infinitely larger. In Koch's words, "Madhouses have been populated by responses to lighter intellectual burdens" (p. 64), and we may be forgiven then for manifesting a very human response to a mind-boggling problem—repressing it.

It would seem the repression was manifest in two ways. One way, taken by a goodly number of psychologists, was to keep their eyes and minds fixed on the white rat or his counterpart in a cage for these many years. The other was to study human behavior in the human, but to confine him in a laboratory cage and treat him pretty much as if he were a rat.

Why, then, are we now so eager to learn what subjects are *really* feeling and thinking? The answer, probably, is that psychology has less need to be defensive about its existence. At least superficially, in numbers and influence, we have progressed enormously in this century, and if we have not developed a coherent science, we have done a masterful public relations job to that effect. Psychology's identity crisis is about over. No one seriously questions if it is here to stay and no rational university administrator would attempt to relegate us back to philosophy or biology. If for no other reason, the potential loss of training and research grant funds would be formidable. The integrity of the discipline is inviolate, and the heretic who asks fundamental questions about the validity of our experimental methods can be tolerated.

A student and seasoned subject once said to me, with apparent innocence: "If everyone does things in experiments for the same reasons I do, I don't understand how you can find out anything that's true." I liken her to the child in the fable, to whom we may now say: "Yes, the Emperor is naked."

2

Role-Related Motives of the Psychological Subject

THE "GOOD" SUBJECT: COMPLIANCE WITH DEMAND CHARACTERISTICS

The motive which has been most commonly attributed to psychological subjects is the motive to comply with the experimenter's expectations. As noted in the previous chapter, Titchener, as early as 1901, warned about subject compliance as a source of artifact, but not until Orne's (1962) paper, "On the social psychology of the psychological experiment: With particular reference to demand characteristics and their implications," did the notion evoke widespread attention.

Orne became concerned with subject compliance after trying without success to find a task that subjects would refuse to work at for prolonged periods of time, which he wanted to use in studies of hypnotic control.

> . . . one task was to perform serial additions of each adjacent two numbers on sheets filled with rows of random digits. In order to complete just one sheet, the subject would be required to perform 224 additions! A stack of some 2,000 sheets was presented to each subject—clearly an impossible task to complete. After the instructions were given, the subject was

deprived of his watch and told, 'Continue to work; I will return eventually.' Five-and-one-half hours later, the *experimenter* gave up. In general, subjects tended to continue this type of task for several hours with little decrement in performance. (p. 777)

Orne persisted in his quest, adding the instruction to subjects that they tear each worksheet into a minimum of 32 pieces before proceeding to the next. Subjects were more persistent, however, continuing at this bit of nonsense for several hours with "little sign of overt hostility."

This uncomplaining compliance, Orne concluded, was a manifestation of the subjects' "identification with the goals of science in general and the success of the experiment in particular. We might well expect then," he maintained, "that as far as the subject is able, he will behave in an experimental context in a manner designed to play the role of 'good subject' or, in other words, *to validate the experimental hypothesis*" (p. 778).

"Demand characteristics" is Orne's term for "the totality of cues which convey an experimental hypothesis to the subject" (p. 779). "An" is a critical word in this definition. A point occasionally misunderstood by later writers is that demand characteristics is a *phenomenological* construct and refers to the *subject's* construction of cues—the hypothesis that the *subject* derives. Disguising those demands which pertain to the true hypothesis does not insure that subjects will not respond in a homogeneous way to some set of cues. Orne's contention is that subjects are deeply motivated to discover the experimenter's intent and will generally assign some meaning to the experiment.

"These cues," he continues, "include the rumors or campus scuttlebutt about the research, the information conveyed during the original solicitation, the person of the experimenter, and the setting of the laboratory, as well as all explicit and implicit communications during the experiment proper. A frequently overlooked, but nonetheless very significant source of cues for the subject lies in the experimental procedure itself, viewed in the light of the subject's previous knowledge and experience. For example, if a test is given twice with some intervening treatment, even the dullest college student is aware that some change is expected, particularly if the test is in some obvious way related to the treatment" (p. 779).

Rosenthal's (1963, 1966) pioneering investigation of "experimenter-expectancy effects" revealed another potent source of demand characteristics, the unintentional, covert communication of expected responses to the subjects by the experimenter. More will be said of these studies in later chapters.

Suppose then, that, in a given experiment, demand characteristics which relate to the hypotheses are eliminated and the data are still in the predicted directions. May we then have confidence that the results were not a function of subject compliance?

It would seem that any attempt to control for demand characteristics is preferable to no attempt. Controls, however, can only be applied to demands which the *experimenter* perceives, which will generally be less than the *subject* perceives. Despite the best attempts of the experimenter to resolve his problem, subjects will keep working on *their* problem of attaching some meaning to the experiment. The researcher is always left with the question of whether there were demands of which he was not aware or, in some cases, which he may have even created by his control procedures.

For example, Freedman and Sears (1965) designed a clever study to test the hypothesis that distraction increases persuasion. The distraction manipulation was to ask subjects to pay attention to the personality of the speaker during his presentation. Though subjects may have been successfully diverted from the notion that they were being intentionally distracted, might they not have pondered why the experimenter called their attention to the speaker's personality and then asked for their opinions about the content of his talk? Might they not readily have concluded that the experimenter was trying to demonstrate that aspects of the speaker's personality, such as his sincerity, self-confidence, etc., would help persuade them?

Related also to the question of the efficacy of controlling for demands is the fact that most, if not all, areas of psychological research are in the inductive and exploratory rather than the deductive stage of inquiry. As a consequence, researchers tend to give as much attention to findings which were incidental or even contradictory to their hypotheses as to those which were predicted. Psychologists have become astute at interpreting any differences among experimental conditions that they observe, and journals are replete with ex-post-facto analyses of effects that were not accounted for or counter to the theories which spawned the experiments. Inasmuch as different experimental conditions may readily harbor different demand characteristics, significant effects of some sort may be commonly obtained in psychological studies. Thus, procedures for disguising hypotheses-related demands do not sizably increase our confidence, in general, about the veracity of psychological data.

THE PRIDEFUL SUBJECT— EVALUATION APPREHENSION

Another facet of the subject's role-related behavior, referred to by Rosenzweig in 1933 as "pride," attained conceptual respectability some 30 years later in Rosenberg's (1965) term "evaluation apprehension." He defined this as "an active anxiety-toned concern that he (the subject) win a positive evaluation from the experimenter or at least that he provide no grounds for a negative one."

Evaluation apprehension seems a very plausible concept of subject motivation if we consider the degree to which psychology is intertwined with psychoanalysis in most people's minds. The notion probably prevails among subjects that our primary concern in experiments is to discover things about them which they find too ego-threatening to discover or reveal about themselves. However exaggerated this idea may be, the fact is that psychologists do tend to study needs and motives and behavioral processes of which people are not readily aware and often would not find completely acceptable.

Probably anyone who has spoken at some length to subjects about their underlying motives has acquired a sense of the scope and pervasiveness of evaluation apprehension. One subject told me that he was kept in the waiting room for an experiment for about ten minutes, whereupon he memorized every object in the room "in case they were going to test me on my alertness." Another described his responses to a Rorschach test: "On one card I saw vaginas all over, but I wasn't going to tell him (the examiner) that; I said they were caves." A well-seasoned subject summarized his experiment-behavior this way: "After a while I just wanted to find out what the experimenter wanted to prove I couldn't do, so I could prove that I could." And a colleague related to me his distress at overhearing a group of males, waiting for his experiment, conclude with much certainty and satisfaction that his attractive lady assistant strutting up and down the corridor on her chores was the independent variable. He decided it was probably useless to discard this group's data; after all, he did not know what was in the corridor when he was not watching.

Rosenberg and his colleagues (Rosenberg, 1969) have reported a series of experiments demonstrating motives based on evaluation apprehension. In these studies the magnitude of evaluation apprehension was manipulated in different subject groups in a variety of ways (e.g., by having the experimenter relate or not relate the study to clinical psychology). In addition, subjects were cued as to what type of response was considered "normal," with the direction of the cued responses varied in different conditions. The test of effects resided in the interactions between evaluation apprehension manipulations and cued directions.

One of these experiments will serve as an illustration. The subjects' task was to rate their liking or disliking of 15 people and their estimates of their "success" and "intelligence" from photographs. Evaluation apprehension was manipulated by having two separate "Background Information Sheets." For the high apprehension condition, this sheet described the study as the "Personality Assessment Project" and went on to state "those photographs comprise a recently developed *Test of Psychological Maturity*. The pattern of responses given to these photographs by psychologically mature undergraduate students has been shown to be significantly different from the responses of those manifesting psychological maladjustment." In the low apprehension form the study was called the "Mathematical Psychology Project," and subjects were told that the experimenters were "interested in integrating the various dimensions or factors involved in social perceptual processes into a more simplified model by a method which statisticians term 'stochastic-inferential mathematical modeling.' "

One-third of subjects in each of these conditions was told by written communication that previous research showed that most people tended to *like* the photos; one-third were informed that most people *disliked* the photos; and the remaining third were given no information. Thus, groups within conditions were formed with *positive response direction cueing, negative response direction cueing,* and *no cueing.*

Table 2 reveals clearly the effects of both cueing and evaluation apprehension manipulation on like-dislike ratings. Subjects tended to like or dislike the photos as they were cued, and this effect was magnified with high evaluation apprehension.

In a separate analysis of the groups who received positive or negative cueing only (eliminating the two control groups) the interaction between evaluation apprehension and response cueing was significant at $p < .03$. Similar analyses of the success and intelligence ratings showed that differences paralleled those for liking, and the interaction terms reached $p<.12$ and $p<.19$, respectively.

Table 2.* Like-dislike mean sums for groups, and probabilities of differences between-groups

	Liking treatment		Control		Disliking treatment
			p .0002		
High evaluation apprehension	+33.50	p. 02	+5.42	p .004	–19.93
	p .05		N.S.		N.S.
Low evaluation apprehension	+13.67	N.S.	+2.83	p .05	–12.00
			p .003		

*There was an additional variable in this study; whether or not the experimenter was a "gatekeeper" for future rewards of the subject; that is, he announced to half the subjects that he would be recruiting participants for an interesting and remunerative student discussion group after the experiment. The prediction that subjects in the gatekeeper condition would show more effects of evaluation apprehension manipulation was not borne out—trends were essentially alike in both conditions—thus, the data shown in Table 2 are for non-gatekeeper subjects only.

Source: Rosenberg, M.J. in Rosenthal and Rosnow (1969). Reprinted by permission.

EVALUATION APPREHENSION AND THE SOCIAL DESIRABILITY RESPONSE SET

The "social desirability response set" (SD) refers to the tendencies of subjects to ascribe to themselves socially favorable aspects of behavior and deny unfavorable aspects on self-rating psychological inventories, particularly personality and attitude tests. It is sometimes called, "faking good."

Again, it was Rosenzweig in 1934 who first expressed serious concern with this source of artifact, but it was not until the late 1950's (Edwards, 1957; Crowne & Marlowe, 1960) that investigators came to appreciate its magnitude. Currently, most self-rating tests have built-in "lie-scales," the scores from which are correlated with other subscales of the test to measure the variance attributable to socially desirable responding. There are also several independent SD scales for this purpose. Items for SD scales deal with typical human fallibilities; common imperfections of behavior from a social desirability standpoint (e.g., *I sometimes feel resentful if I don't get my way. Before voting I thoroughly investigate the qualifications of all the candidates*).

It would appear that this mode of responding to tests is one manifestation of evaluation apprehension, and that subjects high in SD should show more apprehension in general in psychological experiments. One set of findings (Shulman & Silverman, 1974), however, point to the *opposite* relationship.

This study was based on the generally held concept (Crowne & Marlowe, 1964) that SD is a function of an "approval motive." Shulman and Silverman attempted to explore this concept further, by determining whether high SD subjects as compared to lows had a greater *need for approval* or *need to avoid disapproval* or *both*.

Subjects scoring in the top and bottom thirds of the distribution of Marlowe-Crowne SD Scale scores (Crowne & Marlowe, 1960) were recruited to participate in a "study of psychological abilities," in which they were administered parts of various subtests of the Wechsler Adult Intelligence Scale (Wechsler, 1958). By varying the items and times allotted for the tasks, half the subjects in each group were led to believe they had performed either very well or poorly.

Then the experimenter, a graduate student, informed the subject: "Dr. Shulman had planned to be available to discuss your performance at this time, but an unexpected meeting was called. Dr. Shulman did suggest that anyone who wished to discuss their results could make an appointment to see him with his research assistant— Mrs. Tanis—whose office is down the hall."

The experimenter noted, surreptitiously, whether the subject headed for Mrs. Tanis' office or the exit. (Then subjects were called back and told the nature of the study.)

In the *failure* condition, nine of the 22 high SD subjects, compared to three of 22 low SD subjects, went to make an appointment for an evaluation, a difference significant at p<.001. In the *success* condition, nine of 22 highs, compared to 15 to 22 lows, sought an appointment, a difference which reached p<.15. Thus, there was evidence that low SD subjects tended more than highs to avoid disapproval, and a suggestion, also, that they tended more to seek approval. In both regards, it seems to be the low and not the high SD scorer who had more evaluation apprehension.

The resolution of these unexpected data may reside in the percepts of subjects taking an SD test. The underlying assumption of the test is that the subject responds to it as some measure of the "goodness" or social desirability of his behavior. Subjects may readily perceive, however, that items such as: *I have never intensely disliked anyone; On occasion I have had doubts about my ability to succeed in life; No matter who I'm talking to I'm always a good listener;* particularly if they require true or false answers, are designed to measure their honesty and willingness to admit to common human foibles. On this basis, it is the subject who scores *low* who is, in a larger sense, presenting himself favorably on this test by giving testimony to his own self-insight and openness. The findings, then, that low SD scorers are more concerned than highs with gaining approval and avoiding disapproval from the experimenter becomes comprehensible.

And we are alerted, also, to the need for careful consideration of extraneous subject motives even when we are measuring extraneous subject motives.

These notions may help to clarify a paradoxical pattern of data within some of Rosenberg's (1969) studies on the differential effects of "response-cueing" on high and low SD subjects. In one experiment (not the one described previously) in which subjects were required to indicate their liking for people from photos, response-cueing involved telling them that prior studies had shown that "psychologically mature and healthy people" tended either to like or dislike strangers. A "no-cueing" condition served as a baseline measure. High SD subjects showed significantly greater effects of cueing than lows in both conditions. In the "dislike" condition, in fact, lows tended to go *counter* to the cues (p<.10).

In another experiment, subjects were required to perform pages of routine addition problems. Response-cueing entailed saying that previous studies showed that psychologically mature people found the tasks pleasurable and were efficient at them or the converse. Subjects were free to stop whenever they pleased, and the criterion measures were: number completed; number correct; and proportion correct of completed. There was a significant effect of cueing for increased performance on the last measure, but no difference in this effect between high and low SD subjects. In the decreased performance condition, however, lows showed significantly greater cueing effects than highs on all three measures.

Thus, in four separate conditions of response-cueing, there were four different patterns of effects for high versus low SD subjects. These are summarized below:

Response-cueing	*Effects by SD level*
1. Psychologically mature people tend to dislike strangers.	Highs showed effects. Lows showed countereffects.
2. Mature people tend to like strangers.	Highs showed greater effects than lows.
3. Mature people tend to enjoy and are more efficient at routine addition problems.	Highs and lows showed equivalent effects.
4. Mature people tend not to enjoy and are less efficient at routine addition problems.	Lows showed greater effects than highs.

The critical variable differentiating these conditions may be the *credibility* of the response cues, which seem to range markedly from (1) to (4). Subjects probably found it difficult to believe that psychologically mature people have an aversion to strangers. It might have seemed more plausible, but not very much more, that mature people tend to like strangers. Subjects probably assumed, as would the writer, that mature people reserve judgment of someone in a photograph. Similarly, it seems possible but not likely that mature people enjoy routine addition tasks. It is likely, on the other hand, that they tend to dislike such tasks, particularly in the mind of the subject who likes to think of himself as mature and finds in actual practice that he is quite bored.

Thus the low SD subject, because he is more concerned with the purposes of the psychologist's procedures and in performing in a way that does himself credit, gives response opposite to the experimenter's cues when he thinks the information given him is patently untrue (and, perhaps, that the experimenter is testing his rote conformity). When he fully accepts the information, he responds more in accordance with the cues than his high SD counterpart. Areas between these extremes elicit responses between.

This more elaborate interpretation of SD scores may pertain as well to some other contradictory data regarding this variable. Crowne and Marlowe (1964) report that high SD subjects show more opinion change in response to persuasive messages than lows, which is congruent to their interpretation of SD as an expression of approval need. Silverman, Ford, and Morganti (1966), however, found in the opposite direction.

It would seem that this relationship should be sturdier than this, but as Silverman and Shulman (1970) suggest "attitude change studies tend to put subjects in dilemmas. In the subject's mind, there are probably equally salient negative and positive aspects of persuasibility. It may be associated with rank conformity, weak-mindedness and dependence, or with openness, flexibility and responsiveness to new information" (p. 90).

There are a host of extraneous variables in attitude-change studies that could lead subjects to one or the other conclusion: the context of the experiment, the sources of the messages, their plausibility, etc. Thus, low SD subjects, being more responsive to cues regarding the meaning of their behavior in the experiment, would be expected to show either more or less persuasion than highs, depending on the nature of these cues.

EVALUATION APPREHENSION AND COMPLIANCE WITH DEMANDS

Both of these motives—favorable self-presentation and compliance with the experimenter's expectations—seem to be determinants of subjects' laboratory behavior. Writers have generally regarded them as separate and independent motives and have on occasion commented on the predominance of one or the other.

Thus, Orne (1962) has said: "Admittedly, subjects are concerned about their performance in terms of reinforcing their self-image; nonetheless, they seem even more concerned with the utility of their performances."

Rosenberg (1965), in his first paper on evaluation apprehension, considered that Orne's views were "not in conflict with, nor are they particulary close to" his own. Four years later, however, with the benefit of his additional investigations, he stated: "Orne might be interpreted as saying that positive self-evaluation is being sought by the subject, particularly in that he may take pleasure in viewing himself as a helpful and accommodating person. But the present studies . . . suggest that evaluation comprehension focused upon the experimenter is a more potent and more basic pattern of subject sensitivity" (1969, p.344).

Silverman (1965) took a more integrative approach to the question. He maintained, as Rosenberg, that evaluation apprehension was the major aspect of subject motivation, but, also, that compliance with demands could often be attributed to this motive—that is, in the absence of specific cues to the subject as to what sort of response will put him in the most favorable psychological light, he will tend to do what he perceives the experimenter expects him to, on the assumption that typical behavior is normal behavior.

According to Silverman:

> . . . there is a more salient reason for the subject's compliance with demand characteristics, and this relates to what Milton Rosenberg has called 'evaluation apprehension.' We might agree that many people, and especially the late adolescents that usually turn up as subjects, have qualms about the normalcy of some aspect of their psychological life. We might further agree that most people, including the people who serve as subjects, are quite misguided about the powers and interests of psychologists. To their minds we can very casually probe into the most secret and sinful recesses of their psyches, and uncover whatever it is they need to keep covered. It is not surprising, then, that the subject is well motivated to do what he thinks the experimenter thinks he ought to, for deviance from the experimenter's expectations, to many of these subjects, may imply deviance in the clinical sense. (p. 6)

One implication of this reasoning, considered Silverman, is that "very minor changes in the context of an experiment might readily increase or decrease the tendency to respond to demand characteristics. The manner of the experimenter, the wording used to explain the purpose of the study, the ambiguity of this explanation—any of these might affect the level of anxiety of the subject about not doing the normal thing" (p. 6).

A study by Minor (1970) provided some support for these notions. He used a task developed by Rosenthal (1963) to study the subjects' compliance with covert, unintentional cues by the experimenter regarding his expectations. Subjects were asked to rate "the degree of success or failure experienced by individuals pictured in a series of ten photographs" (which had been preselected in pilot study for their neutrality on this dimension). Different groups of experimenters were led to believe that either success (an average of about +5) or failure (an average of about —5) ratings were expected by the investigator. In addition, the introductory remarks to the subjects were designed to induce either low or high evaluation apprehension. In the former condition they were told they were a "standardization group," to obtain an estimate of how accurate these judgments could be made from photographs. In the latter condition they were told that the validity of their social perceptions, which was one index of psychological adjustment, was being measured.

The results, shown in Fig. 1, revealed convincingly that subjects' responses were related to experimenters' expectancies (at p<.01) *only* when evaluation apprehension was raised. Thus, as far as this study is evidence, the desire to demonstrate "normalcy" and not, as Orne states, the wish to make the experiment successful, seems to be the basis for compliance with experimenter demands.

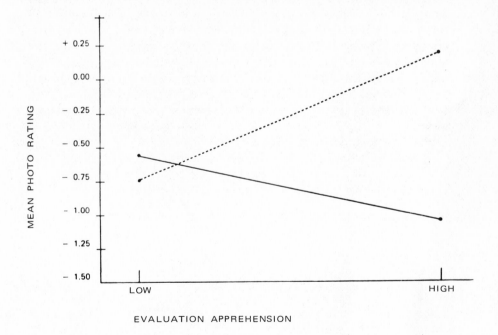

Fig. 1. Mean photo rating by expectancy group and evaluation apprehension level. ——————-5 Expectancy   - - - - - - - - - - +5 Expectancy
Source: Minor (1970). Copyright © 1970 by the American Psychological Association. Reprinted with permission.

Another implication of Silverman's interpretation is that when favorable evaluation and compliance with demands require conflicting responses, the subject will tend to protect his own image rather than the experimenter's. Consider Orne's subjects, who worked hour after hour on nonsense tasks. Were they, as Orne suggested, motivated to comply with the experimenter's expectations? When these subjects were questioned about the tasks, he reports "they would invariably attribute considerable meaning to their performance, viewing it as an endurance test or the like." In a larger sense, then, these subjects were working hard *not to comply* with the experimenter's desires. They were trying to surpass whatever limits to their frustrations or endurance the experimenter expected; to demonstrate their *own superiority to his expectations.*

A direct test of the question of which motive is more salient when the two are in conflict was undertaken by Sigall, Aronson, and Van Hoose (1970). These investigators had subjects perform a tedious task (copying phone numbers) as part of an alleged study in industrial psychology. Subjects were told, "not to rush—to work at a normal rate." All subjects had a seven-minute "practice trial," followed by a brief rest and a seven-minute "real trial." In two other conditions, prior to the second trial the experimenter indicated the approximate rate per minute he expected, which was arranged (by adding or subtracting from the subject's practice rate) to represent either increased or decreased output. In a fourth condition, in addition to stating an expectancy which entailed decreased output, he added that people who tend to rush at a task such as this were probably obsessive-compulsive.

Table 3 shows the mean changes in output between trials for all conditions. All comparisons were significant at $p < .01$, with the exception of Increased Output versus Decreased Output.

Table 3. Mean change in output from "Practice" to "Real" trial

Condition	Mean
Control	+1.9
Increased- Output	+5.7
Decreased Output	+6.2
Decreased Output— Obsessive-Compulsive	–8.0

Source: Sigall, Aronson, and Van Hoose (1970). Reprinted by permission.

Thus, subjects speeded their performances in the Increased Output Condition and slowed in the Decreased Output Obsessive-Compulsive Condition, whereby in both cases these behaviors were congruent to the experimenter's expectancies and also enhanced the subjects' own images. In the Decreased Output Condition, however, when the experimenter's expectations were opposed to the subjects' needs to show capable performance, they responded in a manner counter to demands.

Because psychologists have had an affinity to study *negatively toned behaviors* (e.g., aggression, authoritarianism, conflict, conformity, dependency, etc.), it follows that in many experiments evaluation apprehension and compliance with demands require conflicting responses. In the chapters to come we will see numerous illustrations of this conflict demonstrating, in most cases, the predominance of the need for favorable personal evaluation.

THE PERVERSE SUBJECT—NEGATIVE RESPONDING

There are reasons why a subject may respond counter to demands other than in the interests of favorable self-presentation. He may do so out of sheer perversity.

We are not referring here to the disinterested subject, whose primary mission is to respond in any way that takes him out of the laboratory with the least expenditure of time and energy. This type usually contributes random error variance to data. In contrast, the negative responder is very involved in what the experiment is about and what the experimenter would like him to do, so that he can do the opposite. He is more likely to provide systematic error variance.

The motives for subject perversity are not difficult to envision. Argyris (1968) likened the negative responding subject to the low status employee who tries to "beat the management," and the analogy probably understates the case.

Rarely will we find as unequal a distribution of power as the experimenter-subject relationship. The experimenter is omnipotent. He possesses all the rights, keeps all the secrets, gives all the orders. The subject . . . is a *Subject:* "Their's not to reason why/Their's but to do or die" (or at least, in many instances, receive electric shock). It is totalitarianism, and we know what happens in a totalitarian condition when the subjugated become aware of their own sources of power. There is a revolution; the powers that be are overthrown and the system is overturned. In this more subdued circumstance the subject does not physically overthrow the experimenter, but he may well attempt to overturn the experiment. Consider the following excerpts from a hypothetical letter* written by Jourard (1968), titled "From S to E."

> Dear E [Experimenter]:
> My name is S. You don't know me. I have another name my friends call me by, but I drop it, and became S No. 27 as soon as I take part in your research. I serve in your surveys and experiments. I answer your questions, fill out questionnaires, let you wire me up to various machines that record my physiological reactions. I pull levers, flip switches, track moving targets, trace mazes, learn nonsense syllables, tell you what I see in inkblots—do the whole barrage of things you ask me to do. I have started to wonder why I do these things for you. What's in it for me? Sometimes you pay me to serve. More often I have to serve, because I'm a student in a beginning psychology course, and I'm told that I won't receive a grade unless I take part in at least two studies; and if I take part in more, I'll get extra points on the final exam. I am part of the Department's 'Subject-pool.'
> When I've asked you what I'll get out of your studies, you tell me that, 'It's for Science.' When you are running some one particular study, you often lie to me about your purpose. You mislead me. It's getting so I find it difficult to trust you. I'm beginning to see you as a trickster, a manipulator. I don't like it.
> In fact, I lie to you a lot of the time, even on anonymous questionnaires. When I don't lie, I will sometimes just answer at random, anything to get through with the hour, and back to my own affairs. Then, too, I can often figure out just what it is you are trying to do, what you'd like me to say or do; at those times, I decide to go along with your wishes if I like you, or foul you up if I don't. You don't actually say what your hopes or hypotheses are; but the very setup in your laboratory, the alternatives you give me, the instructions you offer, all work together to pressure me to say or do something in particular. It's as if you are whispering in my ear, 'When the light comes on, pull the *left* switch,' and then you forget or deny that you have whispered. But I get the message. And I pull the right or the left one, depending on how I feel toward you.
> You know, even when you are not in the room—when you are just the printed instructions on the questionnaire or the voice on the tape recorder that tells me what I am supposed to do—I wonder about you. I wonder who you are, what you are really up to. I wonder what you are going to do with the 'behavior' I give you. Who are you going to show my answers to? Who is going to see the marks I leave on your response-

---

*From Jourard, S.M. *Disclosing man to himself.* Princeton, N.J.: D. Van Nostrand, Copyright © 1968 by Litton Educational Publishing, Inc.

recorders? Do you have any interest at all in what I think, feel, and imagine as I make the marks you are so eager to study and analyze? Certainly, you never ask me what I mean by them. If you asked, I'd be glad to tell you. As a matter of fact, I do tell my roommate or my girl friend what I thought your experiment was about and what I meant when I did what I did. If my roommate could trust you, he could probably give you a better idea of what your data (my answers and responses) mean than the idea you presently have. God knows how much good psychology has gone down the drain, when my roommate and I discuss your experiment and my part in it, at the beer-joint. . . .

Did you ever stop to think that your articles, and the textbooks you write, the theories you spin—all based on your data (my disclosures to you)—may actually be a tissue of lies and half-truths (my lies and half-truths) or a joke I've played on you because I don't like you or trust you? That should give you cause for some concern.(pp. 10-11)

Silverman (1965) conjectured that forced participation in experiments may help to create negative-responding subjects. He related an incident involving a graduate student collecting data on angle estimation. Subjects were asked to estimate the degree of angular movement of one arm under one condition in which she moved their arms and another in which they moved their own arms until she told them to stop. Her prediction was that estimates would be more accurate in the latter condition because of additional proprioceptive feedback. The first 18 subjects, volunteers from a class she was teaching, confirmed the hypothesis at a statistically significant level ($p < .05$). The next 13 subjects were meeting part of the Introductory Psychology course requirement for participation, and their data were significant in the opposite direction. There are, of course, several alternative interpretations of this difference, but, among them, the possibility that non-volunteers were deliberately behaving counter to demands.

This view is substantiated in a report by Argyris (1968), of an evaluation of a general psychology course by 600 students. "In many cases," he states, students admitted that they vented their anger about the research participation requirement by "beating the research."

On the other hand, Gustav (1962) presented an anonymous sentence-completion item to her introductory psychology students which read: "When the teacher announced that each student would have to be a subject in an experiment. . . ." She reported that less than a quarter of her sample experienced annoyance about the requirement, and we may assume that not all of these would manifest their irritation by negative responding. Of course, feelings might be somewhat different for the student entering his third or fourth required experiment.

Studies by Cook et al. (1970), and Silverman et al. (1970), have shown that subjects who have been previously deceived and debriefed (explained the nature of the deception) tend more to give responses counter to demands. In both of these reports the effects were attributed to feelings of anger and frustration at being once deceived. Silverman et al. considered also the possibility that "Deceived subjects may have become so alerted to possible further deceptions that they tended to respond counter to any cues regarding the experimenter's hypothesis. An element of gamesmanship may enter the experimental situation in that subjects become wary of 'tricks' underlying the obvious, and do not want to be caught in them" (p. 210).

Orne (1962) takes a more socially optimistic view of the motives of the negative responder. Compliance with demands, he contends, is a largely implicit, non-conscious process. The subject maintains the illusion to himself as well as to the experimenter that he is being as honest and objective as possible in his responses. Thus, if "the demand characteristics are so obvious that the subject becomes fully conscious of the expectations of the experimenter, there is a tendency to lean over backwards to be honest," with the consequence of "biasing in the opposite direction."

To what extent does negative responding occur? Probably considerably less than the self-redeeming and compliant behaviors described previously, as the evidence in the following chapters will suggest. Nevertheless, many subjects, acting out of anger or for other reasons, deliberately do what they perceive the experimenter does not want them to at least some of the time.

3

Role-Related Motives and Psychological Data: Involuntary Behavior

In this and the following chapter I will describe studies which illustrate how role-related subject motives confound experimental observations in diverse areas of psychological research.

Although most of the available findings were included, these are not intended to represent the totality of artifact in psychological methods. A large majority of studies were reported in the last decade or so by investigators working for the most part on their own topics of specialization. The yield of this limited effort suggests, in fact, that every area of human psychological research is vulnerable to some extent to these sources of error.

I have tried to place in this chapter studies dealing with so-called "involuntary" behavior, including those in which subjects' responses are assumed to be beyond deliberate control (e.g., hypnosis, psychophysiological measures), as well as those in which responses are considered to be voluntarily given but not based on conscious design (e.g., verbal conditioning, perception). In Chapter 4 I deal with behaviors which are regarded as *more* voluntary in origin and expression.

This is more of a literary division than a natural boundary, and overlap does occur.

HYPNOSIS

It is generally considered that hypnosis produces an "altered state of consciousness" (White, 1941) in which the subject performs in passive, rote fashion the commands of the hypnotist. Based on this premise, experimenters have used posthypnotic suggestions as manipulations of their independent variables, creating in their subjects whatever self-percepts or other cognitions were desired. For example, Ashley, Harper, and Runyan (1951) hypnotically induced people, at separate times, to believe that they were very rich, or very poor, or themselves and, as the measure of the dependent variable, compared estimates of coin sizes among these conditions. Rosenberg (1960a, b) gave subjects posthypnotic suggestions that their "affective reactions" toward certain attitude objects had changed, in order to test hypotheses about the relationships between affective and cognitive components of attitudes.

This strategy seems almost ideal for putting difficult hypotheses to precise experimental test, in that it enables the experimenter to vary a single aspect of the subject's phenomenological state while leaving everything else intact. It is based, however, on the assumption that the hypnotized subject is responding *only* to the experimenter-hypnotist's suggestions, whereas evidence has been compiled showing that he does, in fact, respond to considerably more.

Fisher (1954) gave 13 subjects in "medium or deep" hypnotic states the suggestion that they would be compelled to scratch their right ears every time they heard the word "psychology." After the subject was awakened, one or more co-investigators entered the room and a general discussion with the subject ensued. Each experimenter spoke the word several times and also attempted, in his questions, to get the subject to do so. It was made apparent to subjects that experimenters were taking note of their ear scratching, and all 13 generally responded according to the suggestion throughout this period.

After about ten minutes of this, experimenters began to chat with the subject about the posthypnotic suggestion itself, and ". . . during the next five or ten minutes every effort was made to create and sustain the impression that the 'experiment' was completed —i.e., that the Es had satisfactorily witnessed the effects of the posthypnotic suggestion, and were now no longer interested in ear scratching behavior per se." During this period the word psychology continued to be mentioned, but just two subjects responded as they had previously. Nine stopped scratching completely, one stopped for awhile and began again, and one held her hand against her ear for the entire time.[1]

Following this, the first experimenter informed the subject that he would presently rehypnotize him and remove the suggestion, thereby intimating that the experiment had not, in fact, been concluded. From that point, seven of the nine subjects who had ceased scratching their ears to the word psychology abruptly resumed.

What is apparent from these findings is that subjects do not respond to posthypnotic suggestions, per se. The stimulus for the subject's response cannot be defined simply in terms of the command given him, but rather in terms of his *percepts of the experimenter-hypnotist's expectations for his behavior.*

As further evidence of this point, Fisher described the individual behaviors of subjects when they were led to believe the experiment was over. "While all the Ss without exception responded in Period 1 when the stimulus word originated from El, four Ss did not respond when they themselves uttered the word; two of these four, moreover, failed to respond when any of the ancillary Es presented the cue . . . five Ss could not be induced to say the word 'psychology' and it is noteworthy that all Ss manifested a decided reluctance to say the word" (p. 504).

Another aspect of interest in this study was the subjects' reactions to a postexperimental interview, when confronted with the fact that they had stopped scratching earlier. "Two . . . offered elaborate 'rationalizations': one said he noticed his ear itching severely everytime the word was mentioned but could not scratch it because his hands were in his pocket (which was untrue); the other claimed he was unable to respond because he had a book in his hands at the time (equally untrue). The remaining seven Ss insisted they did not hear the word mentioned during period 2" (p. 505).

Whatever the bases of these denials, they bear on a conjecture by Orne (1962) that subjects enter with the experimenter into an implicit "pact of ignorance." Subjects will not, Orne says, readily reveal the role-related motives that governed their behavior, though when sufficiently questioned they are often capable of verbalizing these.

If subjects' responses to posthypnotic suggestions are based on

---

[1] These findings were replicated in a similar study by Orne, Sheehan, and Evans (1968).

their percepts of the experimenter's expectations, might not data such as Ashley, Harper, and Runyan's or Rosenberg's be a function of demand characteristics in the experimental designs rather than hypnotic inductions? In a brief study based on this notion, Orne (1959) repeated the Ashley et al. procedure with four subjects, obtaining essentially the same findings (subjects' estimates of coin sizes were largest in the poor condition and smallest in the rich). Then he conducted an extensive postexperimental inquiry whereupon all four subjects correctly described the purpose and hypotheses of the experiment.

In a larger study directed to the same question, Orne (1959) conducted the same procedure with seven hypnotized subjects and 11, selected from the same population, who were instructed to simulate a hypnotic state[2] for the alleged intention of ascertaining whether the experimenter (who was not the hypnotist) could detect who was and was not faking. The findings of Ashley et al. were obtained *both with hypnotized and simulating subjects*, and the data of these two groups were virtually indistinguishable. Further, across both groups, all subjects who showed the expected effects stated the correct hypotheses in the postexperimental inquiry, whereas subjects who did not, with one exception, did not verbalize the hypotheses. The question emerges from this last finding of whether subjects who did not show expected differences were not actually aware of the hypotheses or whether they were, but did not admit it because they had chosen not to comply.

Noteworthy also was the observation that in the postexperimental interview, simulating subjects "readily described their conscious efforts to 'second guess' what the experimenter would expect of them if they were actually in hypnosis." Subjects who verbalized the hypotheses in the hypnotized group, however, tried to maintain their "pact of ignorance" by denying that their notions about the experimenter's expectations had any effect on their responses.

A further study by Orne (1959) showed how subjects' percepts of the experimenter's expectations influence behavior in another aspect of hypnosis—the trance state. Two introductory psychology classes were given demonstrations of hypnosis with three of the

---

[2] In this and subsequent studies (Damaser, Shor, & Orne, 1963; Orne & Evans, 1965, 1966; Shor, 1962; Sutcliffe, 1961) it was established that simulators, if properly motivated, generally cannot be differentiated from hypnotized subjects, even by psychologists trained in hypnosis.

experimenter's confederates serving as subjects. The demonstrations differed solely in that for one class the three subjects manifested catalepsy of the dominant hand only (a behavior which is not known to occur in the absence of a specific suggestion). Then volunteers from both classes were hypnotized and tested for depth of trance by an experimenter who had no knowledge of which demonstration they had attended. Without any suggestion given them, five of nine subjects in the experimental group showed catalepsy of the dominant hand and two showed it in both. In the control group, *none* showed catalepsy of the dominant hand, and three showed it in both (which, according to Orne, was probably due to cues inherent in the test for catalepsy).[3]

On the basis of these observations, Orne conjectured that much of what subjects do in the hypnotic trance may be a function of their concepts about what a hypnotized person is supposed to do. Such descriptions abound, he says, in the media of mass communication as well as available technical sources. In questioning over 200 of his own students, he "failed to find one who did not have a very clear-cut notion about the nature of hypnosis and who could not define the trance in a fashion similar to that found in dictionaries."

In several additional studies, Orne sought to demonstrate that when hypnotized subjects show increases in such things as physical capacity, tolerance for pain, or willingness to commit dangerous or antisocial acts, these too may reflect simply the power of suggestion in the experimental situation.

In one experiment, Orne (1959) measured the amounts of time hypnotized subjects would hold a kilogram weight at arm's length while under the suggestion that the weight was actually resting on a table. Then he showed that with appropriately motivating instructions in the normal waking state, all but one of his nine subjects *exceeded* their performances. In a series of observations reported in the same article, he found that subjects simulating a trance state manifested the same degree of "hypnotic analgesia" to pain inductions customarily used in hypnosis demonstrations (shock, pressure, and heat) as a hypnotized group. Simulators reported that they felt pain but had little difficulty suppressing their reactions.

Finally, Orne and Evans (1965) used simulating and hypnotized groups in a replication of the classic demonstrations by Rowland

[3] This requires placing the subject's hands, one at a time, in various positions. The cataleptic subject behaves as if he has lost voluntary control and his hand remains in the position in which it was placed.

(1939) and Young (1952) that hypnotized subjects will grasp an active rattlesnake, plunge their hands into fuming acid, and throw acid at another person. Both hypnotized and simulating groups followed the suggestions as readily as subjects in the original studies. Apparently, the context of the psychological experiment engenders enough trust in subjects that the welfare of all will be protected, and faith in the purpose of the experimenter's requests, that it is sufficient in itself to elicit these bizarre responses.

Barber (1965, 1970) demonstrated, also, that unhypnotized subjects respond as well as their hypnotized counterparts to eight typical tests of the trance state (e.g., arm levitation, hallucinations, selective amnesia) when told they are tests of "imagination" and given brief motivating talks by the experimenter. Thus, it appears that the hypnotic induction is not a necessary or sufficient antecedent for much of the behavior shown by subjects in hypnosis experiments.

Further, the subject's percepts of the experimenter-hypnotist's expectations is an ever-present source of confounding in hypnosis research. Whether the subject complies with these percepts out of a desire to make the experiment successful, as Orne (1962) suggests, or because he wants to appear as a normally functioning individual is an open question, though Barber and his colleagues have provided some evidence which suggests the latter.

In one study (Barber & Calverley, 1964a) subjects were told that they were being tested for gullibility rather than imagination, which resulted in a sharp drop in responsiveness to the test suggestions described above.

In another experiment (Barber & Calverley, 1964b) nursing students were given two trials of the tests on separate days. For one group, their hospital supervisor told them, prior to the second trial, of rumors that the study had shown that nursing students were "very easily directed" and beseeched them to protect their reputations. This group showed virtually no responsiveness on any of the tests in the second trial, in marked contrast to their first trial and both trials of control groups.

What of hypnotic phenomena outside of the psychological experiment; in clinical settings or as entertainment? One might consider that the same elements of trust and desire to comply exist in these situations as the experiment, elicited by the personage of the physician or clinical psychologist or professional hypnotist.[4]

[4] *See* Barber (1970) for an extended discussion of clinical and stage hypnosis.

Are there any aspects of behavior under hypnosis that go beyond demand characteristics? To ask the question in operational terms: Do hypnotized subjects do anything differently than simulators? Orne (1959) finds that they do, that the nature of hallucinations reported by hypnotized subjects in response to suggestions were notably different than those of simulators. Barber (1970), however, using Orne's criteria for differences, found the hallucinations of both groups to be virtually identical.

Orne, Sheehan, and Evans (1968) gave hypnotized and simulating subjects the suggestion that they would touch their foreheads whenever they heard the word "experiment." When the experimenter used the word unobtrusively, outside of the context of the testing session, simulators had higher rates of response. When the experimenter's secretary did the same, however, hypnotized subjects performed better. The investigators regarded these differences as evidence of some process in hypnosis which represented "essence" rather than artifact, but it may simply have been that simulators, who did not expect the effects to just happen to them, were more vigilant to subtle testing by the experimenter and consequently relaxed their vigilance more when he was not present.

VERBAL CONDITIONING

Many theories about people, particularly in the area of learning, have drawn their evidence largely from studies of rats, which may account for the instant and long-standing popularity of "verbal conditioning" experiments. These provided a precise analogue of operant conditioning procedures used with laboratory animals which could be used with laboratory humans. The procedure consists of the experimenter emitting "social reinforcers," usually in the form of head-nodding or such statements as "good" or "uh-huh," selectively in response to some component of the subject's verbal behavior, and observing increases in the rate of this component. For example, Greenspoon (1955), in what is generally considered to be the forerunner of all verbal conditioning studies, asked subjects merely to "say words" and reinforced plural nouns. Taffel (1955), in a method that became widely used, showed subjects a series of cards, each containing a different verb and the pronouns *I, we, you, he, she,* and *they.* Subjects were asked to construct a sentence for each card using the verb and beginning with any of the pronouns, and were reinforced for sentences beginning with *I* or *we.*

If the concept of conditioning has any heuristic value in explaining what happens to subjects, both human and animal, we might expect that the behaviors "conditioned" in the laboratory bear some predictable relationship to subsequent behavior "in vivo." The rat in the typical operant conditioning study learns to press a bar in his cage for food pellets, but no one, to my knowledge, has ever put a rat so conditioned in an environment approximating his natural habitat to see if he continued to get on his hind legs and press twigs or pipes or other protuberances when he was hungry.

People who keep pets may, in fact, acquire quite a different concept of the processes underlying so-called operant conditioning effects than the operant theorists. For example, my dog, probably like most other dogs, barks and scratches at the door to gain admittance to the house, which would seem to be a prototype of operant learning. In the terms of the model, barking and scratching were "free operants" until they were "reinforced" a sufficient number of times by the "contingency" of door-opening for the animal to reach a predictable "response rate," and that is all the explanation needed to account for the behavior.

If this were a laboratory conditioning experiment, that is all I would see of the dog's behavior and all the explanation I would need to invoke, but since he lives with me I could not help but notice that, probably like most other dogs, he has never barked or scratched at the door to gain admittance unless he had cause to believe that someone was in the house. If everyone is outside and he wants to go inside, he sits quietly at the door and stares at the closest person or runs between the person and the door. If someone is outside and someone is inside, however, he will bark and scratch.

This is not intended to be a treatise on cognition in infrahumans. The point is, however, that the animal's behavior in this situation is based on some considerable awareness on his part of its effects on the people who manipulate his contingencies. The issue is similar for the behavior of the human subject in the verbal conditioning experiment; is he being passively conditioned to emit plural nouns or first person pronouns or whatever, or does he become aware that the experimenter is trying to elicit these responses and decide to comply with demand characteristics?

There have been some studies of the generalization of verbal conditioning effects. A number of these (e.g., Manis & Ruppe, 1969; Sarason, 1958; Scott, 1958; Timmons, 1959) have demonstrated generalization from one task to another *within the context of the experiment*, but, of course, these do not clarify whether conditioning or compliance with demands were at the root of subjects' responses. Most studies of generalization from one context to another have been done in clinical settings, and the results of these, in general, cast some doubt on the conditioning interpretation.

For example, Rickard, Dignam, and Horner (1960) increased the rate of non-delusional speech in a psychiatric patient by reinforcement, but when a new experimenter interviewed the subject the rate dropped sharply until this experimenter, also, began the conditioning procedure. Rogers (1960) reinforced either positive or negative self-referral statements in different groups in a clinical-interview-type situation comprising six sessions per subject. There were predicted differences in verbal behavior between groups within interview sessions, but not outside of these, as measured by pre- and post-scores on a self-description inventory.

On the other hand, Ullman, Krasner, and Collins (1961) reported that psychiatric patients who had been reinforced for "emotional words" by nods and statements of "mmm-hmm" during individual storytelling sessions showed greater progress in group therapy, measured independently, than patients receiving no reinforcement during the individual sessions. Consider, however, that the control condition of this study required that the therapist-experimenter show no expression of interest or approval for four sessions while the patient-subject told his stories (which patient-subjects probably assumed were meaningful indices of their mental states if therapist-experimenters were so interested in them), while conditioned subjects were exposed to at least a minimal amount of affective feedback for their efforts. The depersonalizing experience of control subjects may have so lowered their self-esteem and confidence as to account for differences in group therapy.

Insko (1965) reported a successful generalization of verbal conditioning effects, but these data also have a plausible alternative interpretation, which will be described later in this section.

Most verbal conditioning studies, however, including the very earliest, contained some post-conditioning measure of the subject's awareness, and herein is the most interesting data from the viewpoint of role-related behavior. The early studies used mainly three or four questions which asked subjects, in general, what they thought determined the specific words they used and what they believed was the purpose of the experiment.

Krasner, in 1958, reviewed 31 verbal conditioning studies and found that, by this criterion, approximately 5 percent of the combined total of subjects showed awareness of the relationship of their responses to the experimenters' reinforcement procedures. These 5 percent, naturally, had been excluded from the various data analyses, and the assumption was that the findings for the remaining majority represented conditioning effects.

Levin (1961), however, perhaps anticipating the concept of the "implicit pact of ignorance," administered to subjects in a Taffel-type, sentence-completion, verbal conditioning study, a more extensive interview, which is reproduced below. The first four questions approximated the typical interviews of prior studies.

1. Did you usually give the first sentence which came to your mind?
2. How did you go about deciding which of the words to use?
3. Did you think you were using some of the words more often than others? Which words? Why?
4. What did you think the purpose of this was?
5. What did you think about while going through the cards?
6. While going through the cards did you think that you were supposed to make up your sentences in any particular way?
7. Did you get the feeling that you were supposed to change the way in which you made up your sentences? How?

(If, in answering Questions 1-7, S mentioned the fact that E had said 'good,' Questions 8-10 were not asked since they were designed to investigate S's awareness of the reinforcer.)

8. Were you aware of anything else that went on while you were going through the cards? (If S mentioned 'good,' Questions 9 and 10 were not asked.)
9. Were you aware of anytning about me? (If S mentioned 'good,' Question 10 was not asked.)
10. Were you aware that I said anything?

(If S failed to mention 'good' in answering this question, the interview was terminated since the remaining questions all refer to S's reaction to 'good.' For Control Ss the interview was terminated following this question.)

11. What did my saying 'good' mean to you?
12. Did you try to figure out what made me say 'good' or why or when I was saying 'good'? (If S answered "no," Question 15 followed Question 12.)

13. How hard would you say that you tried to figure out what was making me say 'good'? Very hard? Fairly hard? Not hard at all?
14. What ideas did you have about what was making me say 'good'?
15. Would you say that you wanted me to say 'good' very much? Some? Didn't care one way or the other?
16. While going through the cards did you think that my saying 'good' had anything to do with the words that you chose to begin your sentences? What?

(If S verbalized a correct contingency at any time during the interview, the above schedule was discontinued and the following questions were asked.)

(A) Is that something you were actually aware of while going through the cards or is it something you thought of just now?
(B) Do you remember when, while going through the cards, that idea occurred to you?
(C) Did the fact that you realized this have any effect on the way you make up your sentences? In other words, did you try and make up your sentences in that way because I was saying 'good'?

All Ss who verbalized a correct contingency were also asked Question 15.

A subject was designated as aware by this extended interview if he stated at any time that "good" had followed sentences beginning with I or we or both, and if he indicated in response to Question A that he became cognizant of these contingencies during the experimental trials.

Using the first four questions only, three of 60 subjects were classified aware, which was precisely the 5-percent figure found, overall, in prior studies. With the extended interview there were 16 more, bringing the total to close to a third of the sample. The most compelling data, however, were the verbal conditioning protocols.

Figure 2 compares the distributions of I and we responses of subjects in the conditioning and control (nonreinforced) groups, excluding the 5 percent of subjects who indicated awareness to the standard four-question interview. Differences were similar to those of prior studies and significant at p<.05.

Figure 3, however, shows these distributions for subjects classified aware by the extended interview, subjects unaware, and controls. Obviously, aware subjects accounted for all of the verbal conditioning effects. Their responses differed significantly from both unaware and control groups and differences between the latter did

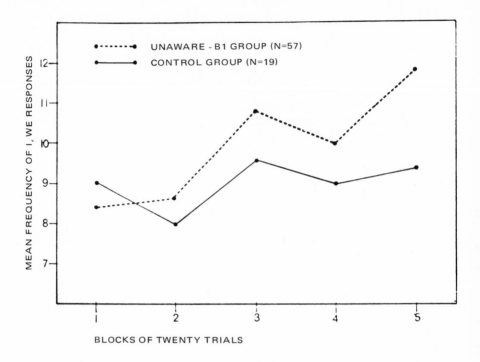

Fig. 2. Mean frequencies of I, we responses for unaware brief-interview (B1) and control groups.

Source: Levin (1961). Copyright © 1961 by the American Psychological
Association. Reprinted by permission.

not approach significance.

To strengthen his case, Levin analyzed separately results for the ten subjects who had indicated knowledge of just one of the two criterion pronouns, showing that increases in response rates occurred only for the pronoun for which the subject was aware.

Levin's findings were soon after replicated in full by Spielberger, Levin, and Shephard (1962) with a college student population. (Levin's study was conducted with hospital patients.)

From a methodological standpoint, the main impact of these findings is not that subjects were more cognizant of contingencies than prior investigators had believed, but that, in study after study, sufficient numbers to generate what appeared to be verbal conditioning effects had pretended ignorance throughout the experimental

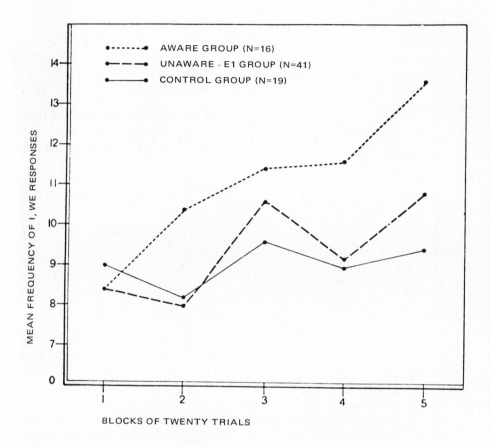

Fig. 3. Mean frequencies of I, we responses for aware, unaware, extended-interview (E1), and control groups.
Source: Levin (1961). Copyright © 1961 by the American Psychological Association. Reprinted by permission.

trials and the postexperimental interview.

It is perhaps difficult to conceive that psychological subjects are so devious, and some might consider the possibility that concepts about the contingencies were implicit and could not be verbalized until the extended interview; that is, subjects had not consciously put it all together about why they had responded as they did until they were adequately prodded and cued by the experimenter.

These doubts, however, were put to rest by two later studies

(Levy, 1967; White & Shumsky, 1972). For half of the samples in each of these experiments, there was no question of whether subjects were or were not aware during the conditioning trials; each was thoroughly briefed beforehand, in the waiting room, by a confederate of the experimenter posing as another subject who had just completed the task.

Summing across the data of both of these reports we find that *not one* of the 48 informed subjects indicated that they had foreknowledge of the contingencies during the conditioning trials or the extended postexperimental interview.[5]

In neither of the studies were the experimenters administering the trials able to ascertain, on a better than chance basis, which subjects had or had not been informed. Both informed and uninformed groups in both studies showed typical conditioning effects. In Levy's, the shapes of the acquisition curves were similar but the overall level of performance was higher for the informed group. White and Shumsky found a trials-by-conditions interaction which suggested that initial frequencies of I and we responses were the same, but informed subjects increased these more rapidly.

In Levy's study, 13 of 16 informed subjects indicated awareness on the postexperimental interview; in White and Shumsky's this figure was 22 of 32, a total across studies of 73 percent. White and Shumsky found no significant difference in the number of items required to elicit statements of awareness between informed and uninformed subjects. Levy reported that informed groups showed awareness *later* in the interview than their uninformed counterparts. When asked directly, after the interview, whether they had prior information about the experiment, one of Levy's and nine of White and Shumsky's informed subjects admitted so, a total of 21 percent.

The fact that 27 percent of subjects who were known to be aware did not reveal this in an extended interview is salient to the interpretation of several findings contradictory to Levin's, and Spielberger, Levin, and Shephard's, to the effect that subjects classified unaware by such an interview nevertheless showed conditioning effects (Bryan & Lichtenstein, 1966; Oakes, 1967). Apparently, a sizable proportion of subjects will be impervious to the best efforts of experimenters to extract admissions of awareness after the fact.

The observation that in some studies subjects classified unaware have shown acquisition effects and in some studies they have not is also interpretable from the results of Levy, and White and Shumsky.

---

[5] This was an abbreviated 12-item form of Levin's, developed by Spielberger and Levin (1962).

Differences in confession rates of informed subjects between these studies suggest that the experimenter and/or other aspects of the experimental situation are significant determinants of whether or not aware subjects will reveal themselves.

Later studies with college students have shown that subject secretiveness is not limited to the verbal conditioning paradigm. In one (Golding & Lichtenstein, 1970), subjects were informed in the waiting room by a confederate posing as another subject about the bogus nature of a heart-rate measure to be used on them. Not one of the 40 informed subjects, all males, volunteered the fact that he had prior information. Responses on the criterion variable were similar between non-informed and informed groups and similar to the findings of prior research with this manipulation (Valins, 1966), that is, subjects rated photos of females higher in attractiveness which they were led to believe had earlier caused their heart rates to accelerate. Subjects were administered a 13-item, postexperiment interview ascertaining their suspicions about the procedure, and overall levels of admitted awareness were low and indistinguishable between informed and non-informed groups.

Newberry (1973) had confederates supply correct answers to 108 female subjects waiting for studies of problem-solving abilities. Again, not one subject voluntarily told her experimenter that she had been coached. Subjects consistently used the information to maximize their performances and, across the various postexperiment interview methods employed by the experimenters, less than 50 percent admitted that they had any prior knowledge about the study.

But what is it about a psychological experiment that turns assumably well-meaning individuals into blatant, notorious liars? If we realize that subjects do not necessarily share their experimenter's passion for authentic data, that they partake, often with reluctance or ambivalence, in a brief, mysterious interaction which has nothing much to do with the rest of their lives, and that they are primarily motivated to get out without creating unpleasantness or appearing foolish, then their behavior becomes very feasible.

Consider the subject in a verbal conditioning study who becomes suspicious. For him to interrupt the task to tell the experimenter that he thinks he has caught on to what is really happening would seem presumptuous at the least. After he complies with demands (or deliberately does not—it is difficult, once demands are apparent, not to do one or the other), to inform the experimenter that he was aware would be admitting that he did not follow instructions (e.g., to say the first word or sentence that came to mind) and that he probably "spoiled the experiment" (a common phrase of subjects who do reveal themselves). Besides, the experimenter, clearly, has not been honest with the subject, and there is no compelling motive for the subject to treat the experimenter differently.

This is likely the essence of the "implicit pact of ignorance" in most situations, rather than Orne's concept of a covert complicity of subjects and experimenters to make the experiment successful. Certainly, Newberry's data suggest that subjects are not very much motivated by the latter concern.

If verbal conditioning experiments have not told us much about verbal conditioning, they have provided an excellent method to study the variables effecting compliance with demand characteristics. For example, studies by Holmes (1967) and Page (1970) showed that experiences as a subject and in psychology courses were related to increases in both awareness and conditioning.

Sheehan (1969) and S. Page (1971) found that conditioning was a direct function of the experimenter's expectancy as to whether it would occur. Videotape analyses by S. Page revealed that experimenters with positive expectancies engaged in a variety of ingratiation tactics which were assumed to elicit subjects' cooperation with demands.

S. Page (1971) showed that a manipulation designed to increase evaluation apprehension, that is, administration of a brief personality test prior to the conditioning trials reduced acquisition effects. Postexperimental interview data suggested that this was not attributable to lesser frequency of awareness but rather to lesser desires to cooperate. Obviously, the personality test, which comprised items related to anxiety, conformity, and need for approval from authority figures, cued subjects that the conditioning task was a measure of their independence and susceptibility to social control. One wonders whether a personality pre-test dealing with such traits as social sensitivity and communication skills would have increased acquisition.

Verbal conditioning studies provide good illustrations, as well, of how role-related behavior can produce spurious results in what Lindgren and Byrne (1971) have called "r-r" (response-response) studies. A common strategy in behavioral research is that, after a construct has been defined and demonstrated, there is a rush of following studies designed to test predictable interactions with inter-subject variables. These relationships, when found, are assumed to increase the validity of the original construct. For example, inverse relationships between verbal conditoning effects and autonomy (Weiss, Ullman, & Krasner, 1960) and independence (Babledelis, 1961) were regarded as evidence that people who were more secure in interpersonal interactions tended less to use social reinforcers as bases for modifying their behavior.

When the evidence for the construct can be readily ascribed to role-related motives, however, as in the case of verbal conditioning, we can often find explanations for correlations with individual difference variables based on these same motives. Thus, it is plausible, particularly in light of the findings by S. Page (1971) described above, that autonomous and independent types were less likely to comply with demand characteristics, particularly when they perceived that these required them to present themselves as conforming and approval-seeking. An alternate possibility is that the relationships were based on latent factors associated with extraneous subject motives; persons high in evaluation apprehension were more prone to *portray themselves* as autonomous and independent on self-rating inventories and were also more likely to deliberately *not* conform to demands when these entailed showing antithetical traits (especially after they had portrayed themselves on the inventories as autonomous and independent). It is not difficult to construct similar explanations for the positive relationships reported between conditioning effects and such variables as susceptibility to hypnosis (Weiss, Ullman, & Krasner, 1960) and need for approval (Crowne & Strickland, 1961).

As in the discussion of hypnosis research, the point is not whether verbal conditioning exists or does not, but that the psychological experiment, as it is generally conceived, is a most unsuitable place to ascertain this.

In several studies by Insko and his colleagues (Insko & Butzine, 1967; Insko & Cialdini, 1969), the usual parameters of the verbal conditioning experiment were extended somewhat. People, unknowing that they were psychological subjects, were contacted by telephone for alleged opinion surveys on topics such as the desirability of pay TV, and were reinforced by the experimenters saying "good" after either pro or con statements. Post-conditioning interviews showed that small fractions of subjects reported awareness of these contingencies and the "unaware" majorities consistently showed acquisition effects.

It is difficult for this reader to conceive that people of normal intelligence were oblivious to the incongruous behavior of a surveytaker who exclaimed "good" every time they voiced an opinion in a certain direction. It is not difficult to conceive, however, that people in other mysterious situations behave much like subjects in psychological experiments, and that many of the interviewees responded to this peculiar pollster, out of curiosity or compliance, by giving the answers which so obviously generated his enthusiasm. It is understandable, also, that they later denied the fact to avoid embarrassment for themselves or simply to extricate themselves from further complications.

In one study, Insko (1965) reinforced opinions about creating a "springtime aloha week" on the University of Hawaii campus by the telephone-survey method, and measured attitudes a week later by questionnaires circulated in classrooms. The issue, however, was specific enough so that respondents would certainly consider that the "pollster-prosyletizers" and those interested in the questionnaire responses were the same group, and generalization effects may have been due, simply, to subjects' desires to show consistency.

Moving the experiment from laboratory to life is a laudable direction, but it is also necessary to leave behind the pervasive preconceptions that people do not think except along the lines explicated by psychological theories.

One verbal conditioning experiment (Rosenfeld & Baer, 1969), provocatively subtitled "The double-agent effect," took an intricate route around the awareness issue. In this study, a graduate student recruited to be an experimenter conducted a series of interviews with another graduate student in which he attempted to increase the base rate of chin-rubbing by selectively nodding his head. The alleged subject was actually the experimenter (the double-agent), who successfully conditioned the interviewer by rubbing his chin each time the latter used "yeah" as a prompt. The nature of this contrivance and the responses by the duped interviewer to the postexperimental inquiry left little doubt that suspicion about contingencies was not a determinant of these results. But to accomplish this the experimenter constructed an event so exotic that one must question whether it is representative, at all, of the construct to which it pertains, and thus whether it can be generalized to any aspect of ongoing human interaction. A situation in which one is employed to try to manipulate some incidental behavior of another who is really a double-agent, using his knowledge of the mission to manipulate an incidental behavior of the first party, does not often arise in the real world, where people are generally what they are supposed to be and doing what we think they are doing.

Aside from the issue of awareness, this question may be raised about most verbal conditioning experiments. Oakes (1972) reports a number of studies in which psychology students who were coerced to be subjects were required to discuss assigned topics in groups of four, and were each selectively reinforced, via earphones, for participation. An attempt to replicate the study with "real people" who volunteered for these discussion groups in response to newspaper ads was unsuccessful, because the people were so interested in each other that "opportunities for participation were being used to the fullest before the reinforcers were introduced."

But even as I compose these paragraphs on the non-veridicality of verbal conditioning data, my mate passes my study and says something to me, and I know that the inflection in my answer is calculated to either encourage or discourage conversation at the moment, and that she is usually responsive to the messages in my para-language, as I am to hers, and that is how we manage to get along. The paradox is that, undoubtedly, something akin to verbal conditioning pervades our day-to-day interactions, though some other conceptual terminology may prove to be more adequate for its description.

Then why is it that not one psychological study on the topic seems to have approached or simulated the conditions under which it occurs so naturally? Perhaps because we did not take a systematic look at the places and people in which it naturally occurs before we developed our theories or experimental analogues.

PSYCHOPHYSIOLOGICAL MEASURES

Researchers who use psychophysiological measures of their criterion variables may feel aloof to the problems of extraneous subject motivation, for it does appear that these mensurational techniques are inviolate to the kinds of bias we have discussed. Nevertheless, there are several studies which show that even these seemingly purest of involuntary responses may be influenced by role-related motives.

A series of reports by Hess and his colleagues (Hess, 1965; Hess & Polt, 1960, 1966; Hess, Seltzer, & Shlien, 1965) created interest in pupillary dilation as an index of the attention or arousal value of a stimulus for a subject. One set of findings with this measure were that males tended to dilate more to sexually provocative pictures of women than of men (Hess & Polt, 1960; Nunnally, Knott, Duchnowski, & Parker, 1967) and that these differences were reversed in a sample of homosexual males (Hess, Seltzer, & Shlien, 1965).

Chapman, Chapman, and Brelje (1969), however, during a pilot study of pupillary responses to sexual stimuli, noticed that different experimenters were obtaining different results. This led them to attempt to replicate the findings of differential dilation by males to photographs of women versus men, using two experimenters who were deliberately selected because of discrepancies in the images they projected and in their styles of interaction.

> E_1 was a 28-yr.-old married male graduate student. He wore a coat and tie and maintained with his Ss a businesslike, somewhat formal, and aloof relationship. His manner appeared to communicate the message that the experiment was a serious affair in which Ss were expected to work carefully and behave properly, much as they are expected to conform and behave properly in a classroom situation. E_2 was a 21-yr.-old male unmarried undergraduate who came to the experiment dressed in khaki trousers and either a sport shirt or pullover sweater. He was an energetic, buoyant, casual young man with a very friendly but 'breezy' approach to interactions with others. His style of deportment communicated fairly immediately an image of a carefree, fun-loving undergraduate, with a lively interest in the opposite sex. He interacted with his Ss as equals, rather than as a superior in the academic hierarchy. (p. 397)

Experimenters were told to behave in their accustomed ways in dealing with subjects, but to present the experiment precisely according to written instructions.

As predicted, the data were similar to prior studies only for the casual experimenter. Subjects seen by the formal experimenter dilated about equally for male and female photographs. It may be that these subjects suffered or imposed constraints on their interest in female anatomy in this non-frivolous atmosphere, or that subjects purposefully show more attentive responses to female photos in contexts where this would seem to be appreciated. In either case, we must conclude that the psychological experiment is unsuitable to answer as basic a question as whether college males enjoy photographs of beautiful nude women more than photographs of men.

The most widely used human psychophysiological measure has been the galvanic skin response (GSR). Ellison, Davis, Saltzman, and Burke (1952) reported a curious finding using the GSR in a study of contrived feedback on "lie detection." Subjects who were told after one trial that their lie had been detected by their GSRs became harder to detect on a subsequent trial, while subjects who were told they had deceived the polygraph became easier to detect.

Orne (1965) was taken by the contradiction between these findings and the experience of actual lie-detector adminstrators, who maintain that respondents must be convinced of the efficacy of the technique for it to be effective. He surmised that the difference may reside in the fact that people taking the test in actual situations obviously have a need *not* to be detected, while subjects in experiments may wish to be revealed to show that they are not practiced liars or simply to comply with expectations.

Orne designed an experiment similar to those of Rosenberg, described in the previous chapter, in which "response cues" were manipulated to instill dispositions in subjects either to be detected or not. One group was informed in the instructions that ". . . it is not possible to detect lying in the case of psychopathic personalities or habitual liars," while another was told ". . . while it is extremely difficult to fool the lie detector, highly intelligent, emotionally stable and mature individuals are able to do so."

Each subject drew a card with a number on it from a deck and then all possible numbers were presented by tape while GSRs were being recorded. The experimenter had independent access to the number selected by the subject, and when the trial was over he gave half in each group the impression they had been detected by calling out that number, and half the impression they had deceived the machine by calling out an incorrect choice.

The data were complex. Subjects given different response cues did not differ in frequency of actual detection on the trial described above, but there was a very powerful interaction between response cues and feedback on detection on a subsequent trial with a new card. Subjects for whom feedback did not match the dispositions that had been given them by the response cues—that is, those who had *wanted* to be detected and were told they *had not been* and those who had wanted *not* to be detected and told they *had been*—became easier to detect. Across both of these groups, 29 of 33 were detected. On the other hand, subjects whose dispositions, either for detection or deception, had been confirmed by the feedback, became harder to detect. Twenty-five of 32 were not detected.

There is a parsimonious explanation of Orne's and Ellison et al.'s findings, as well as the reports of lie-detector administrators in life situations, if we consider that the likelihood of a subject being detected—that is, showing an accelerated GSE to the critical item—depends on his overall level of anxiety about the test. In Ellison et al.'s and Orne's studies the source of the anxiety was irrelevant; both subjects who had the motive to be detected and believed they were not, and subjects who had the motive to deceive and believed they had not, became more anxious about their performances. Subjects who were led to feel they had responded in a way that protected their images tended to relax on the second trial.

The implications are clear for the uses of the GSR in lie-detector research or any other kind. The level of anxiety of the subject about his responses will effect his data, and these anxieties may readily come from the demand characteristics of the situation. Consider a simple hypothetical illustration:

An investigator wants to test a theory about repressed dependency needs and performs a manipulation designed to arouse anxiety about these. Then he tests subjects' GSRs to dependency-related stimuli. Successful data may mean that subjects were anxious for the reasons posited by the investigator *or* that their suspicions about the nature of the experiment made them anxious about their responses to the relevant stimuli. The investigator will probably never know, and, given the data on subject secretiveness related in the previous section, asking them will be of little help.

LEARNING AND PROBLEM-SOLVING

Studies of learning, memory, problem-solving abilities, etc., may appear also to be relatively unconfounded by role-related behavior. Experiments in these areas are usually presented in a straightforward manner untainted by the aura of mystery or contrivance. The implicit assumption is that the subject's concern about his image will be manifest in the motive to give his best possible performance.

But the motives that accrue to the subject role, even in these simplistic situations, may be more complex than this. For example, it has been a fairly consistent finding, dating back more than 40 years, that males are superior to females in problem-solving, particularly for problems requiring quantitative reasoning (e.g., Maier, 1933, Carey, 1958). On the other hand, women have shown superiority to men in studies of verbal learning—short-term memory for series of simple objects, usually three-letter nonsense syllables (Hetherington & Ross, 1963; Littig & Waddell, 1967). It would be easy to conclude that this is at least part of the reason why more males become scientists and more females become secretaries.

It is conceivable, however, that the psychology experiment, with its connotation of psychological evaluation, elicits traditional sex-role stereotypic behavior in learning tasks, and this may be particularly so for female subjects inasmuch as the large majority of experimenters are male (Silverman, 1974). Thus, women may be less motivated than men to demonstrate quantitative reasoning abilities and, at the same time, more inclined than their male counterparts to show tolerance and effectiveness in simpleminded repetitive exercises such as memorizing lists of nonsense syllables.

In support of this position, several studies have shown dramatic variations in sex differences for both of these abilities when the sex of the experimenter is taken into account. With a female experimenter, women become more astute at quantitative problem-solving (Hoffman & Maier, 1966), but their proficiency is lowered on verbal learning tasks (Archer, Cejka, & Thompson, 1961; Littig & Waddell, 1967).

Hoffman and Maier observed further that introductory remarks by a male experimenter in which he stated that he was doing the study to show that women were just as capable thinkers as men had a similar effect of increasing problem-solving in females. Interestingly, the same statements by a female experimenter to female subjects had the effect of decreasing performance.

In addition, in an earlier study, Hoffman and Maier (1961) found that problem-solving performance of women was poorer when tests were conducted in all female rather than mixed-sex groups, perhaps because sex-role identification was made more salient in the former condition.

Sex is not the only attribute of experimenters that interacts with learning and problem-solving, as we will see in a later chapter, and, though most demonstrations of artifact in learning paradigms have been concerned with the nature of the experimenter, it is eminently feasible that other aspects of the learning study engender role-related behaviors as well. There has been less attention to this area of psychology than many others, probably because of the notions discussed in the first paragraph of this section. But the subject who is being scrutinized for whether he performs a "reversible" or "non-reversible shift," or which paired-associates or nonsense syllables he is most likely to remember, is as attuned as any other subject to the possible meanings of his responses for the experimenter's expectations and evaluations. Inasmuch as there has been a paucity of attempts to corroborate the findings of learning experiments in naturalistic situations (Koch, 1969), the issue of subject role behaviors in these studies assumes considerable importance.

PERCEPTION

Psychologists have become somewhat less naive about their subjects since the controversy of the 1950's about whether higher recognition thresholds for "dirty" words were based on "perceptual defense" or people's reluctance to admit that they thought the fleeting tachistoscopic images were "bitch" and "whore" until they were certain (cf. Secord & Backman, 1964). Still, the classic conundrum in perception research is whether the subject reports what he experiences or what he thinks he should experience, and there are several contemporary illustrations of the latter.

The concept of "set" has commanded the attention of perception researchers more than any other notion. In one often cited demonstration of set effects, Harper (1953) had subjects view a series of pictures of objects of the same orange-to-red color, while he varied the background coloration, and report to him when the object merged with the background. To induce color-sets, some were typically red objects (e.g., apple, heart); control objects were not, but were similar in shape to the former (e.g., oval, triangle). In addition, the experimenter described the typically red objects as "reddish" and the others as "yellowish-orange." Findings were as predicted; more background red was required before set-inducing objects were reported to disappear than control objects.

Hendrick, Wallace, and Tappenbeck (1968) conducted a set of studies to see whether Harper's subjects' responses could be attributed to demand characteristics and, further, whether these demands were conveyed by the differential objects or by color naming or both.

These investigators first repeated Harper's procedures, except that the figures used for all conditions were the same, and were described either as objects with or without a specific color typically associated with them. Across these conditions, objects were either called by a color label or were not. For example, a green triangle was presented four times in the series, called: a *tree*, a *triangle*, a *green tree*, or a *green triangle.*

Findings corroborated Harper's and indicated further that *both* object identification and color naming increased set effects independently; that is, the amount of background green required was significantly greater in all conditions compared to the one in which objects were given no color association or label.

Then the authors performed the experiment again, but the figures were *surreptitiously removed* from the background field at a fixed point in the trials. Thus, the objects were made to actually disappear and any differences among conditions could only be attributed to demand characteristics. No such differences occurred for object identification, but there were effects in the expected direction approaching significance ($p<.10$) for color labeling.

Another revelation of artifact in perception research, described by Dodwell and Genreau (1969), concerns the phenomenon of the figural aftereffect (FAE). Discovered by Gibson in 1933, FAEs are demonstrated by having subjects fixate on or near a line or other simple configuration, called the inspection (I) figure, then substituting an appropriate test (T) figure. The T figure is reported to be seen as displaced away from the previous location of the I figure. For example, if the I figure is a slightly curved line, a T figure of a straight line will appear to be curved in the opposite direction.

In 1944, Kohler and Wallach reported a number of studies of FAEs from which they developed the "satiation" principle, an analysis of the neural correlates of form perception in terms of electrical fields. Satiation theory engendered much attention and controversy (cf. Lashley, Chow, & Semes, 1951) and a plethora of following experiments with the FAE.

Dodwell and Genreau were inspired to their investigation as a result of pilot studies they performed with several methods for obtaining FAEs which they planned to use in further research. Their tests were notably unsuccessful; they found that with "experimentally naive subjects" (without prior experience with the procedure or preconceptions about expected effects), "extremely few reports of FAE were obtained at all." *Dodwell, himself,* however, had FAEs which were consistently as expected.

This led them to a careful scrutiny of the literature, from which they concluded that there were "large inconsistencies in the reports of the size and direction of FAEs," and many indications that the phenomenon was related to the sophistication and expectations of the subject.

> To take the classical paper by Kohler and Wallach (1944) as an example, 63 experimental situations were reported . . . in only five cases (for five figures) were the number of subjects and some measure of the size of effect mentioned, and in three of these Kohler and Wallach were mentioned specifically as subjects. . . . Many experiments on FAE have used graduate students or similarly interested participants as subjects . . . a number of investigations on naive observers (e.g., Weitz & Post, 1948; Duncan, 1958) have failed to obtain any evidence of FAEs. (pp. 151-152)

Then Dodwell and Genreau (1969) performed an experiment using the I and T figures shown in Fig. 4. By pressing a button, subjects were able to move the image of Bar A from left to right, which they were asked to do until the distance AB seemed equal to the distance CD. There were ten practice trials, followed by ten control trials without the I figure, followed by ten experimental trials with prior viewing of the I figure, followed by another ten control trials. Prior to the trials, subjects were given one of five levels

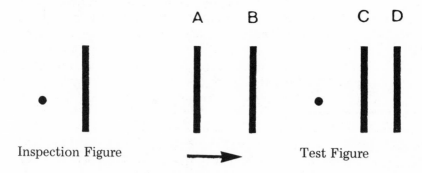

Inspection Figure   ⟶   Test Figure

Fig. 4. Inspection and test figures.
Source: Dodwell and Genreau (1969). Reprinted by permission.

of suggestions—*strong positive*, *positive*, *zero*, *negative*, *strong negative*—described below.*

> By a positive suggestion we mean a suggestion that the FAE will occur in the classically expected direction, namely that after inspection of the I figure the bars AB will be set farther apart than when there has been no such inspection, since inspection causes the distance between C and D to appear to increase. By a negative suggestion we mean the opposite, that is to say that the AB setting will be smaller after inspection, since inspection causes the distance between C and D to appear to decrease.
>
> Identical instructions, in the form of a 'rational' explanation, were read to all the suggestion groups, except that the words 'fatigue'/'warm-up'; 'tired'/'warmed-up'; 'out, away from the tired region'/'in, to take advantage of this warmed up area'; 'farther apart'/'closer together' were appropriately interchanged for positive/negative suggestion. Strong suggestion (positive or negative) consisted of a further statement, identical for both strong suggestion groups, that the expected result was largest for people with high IQs. The zero group received no such instructions. (p. 153)

The FAE score for each subject comprised the mean degrees of adjustment on control trials subtracted from the mean for experimental trials; thus, a negative score corresponded to the negative suggestion and a positive score corresponded to the positive suggestion and represented the classic effect.

Twenty subjects were assigned to each level of suggestion. They were preselected on the basis of a "body-sway" test of general suggestibility (Eysenck, 1947) with ten high and ten low suggestible subjects included in each group. In addition, half of subjects within each of these conditions received the FAE trials under either optimal or less than optimal viewing conditions, achieved by projecting the I and T figures on a semicircular screen to the center (optimal) or toward the periphery (sub-optimal) of the visual field.

There were profound and highly significant effects of suggestion (F = 49.7; p<.001) which are shown in Fig. 5. Mean FAEs were in near perfect linear relationship to levels of suggestion and with zero

*Reprinted by permission.

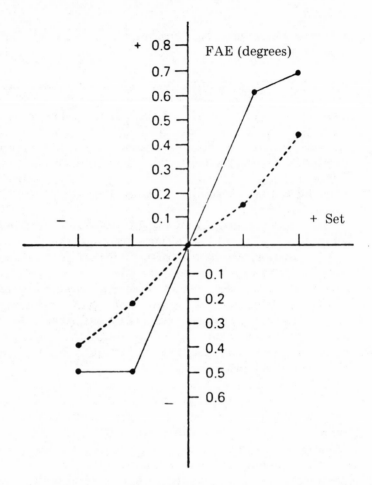

Fig. 5. FAE's as a function of set and viewing conditions. Points on the horizontal axis refer to levels of suggestions.   ----------------- central
                                                                                  ——————— peripheral
Source: Dodwell and Genreau (1969). Reprinted by permission.

suggestion, there was a zero mean FAE.

Suggestion effects were, as predicted, significantly greater in the poorer (peripheral) viewing condition, presumably because of greater ambiguity of the stimuli. High suggestible subjects on the sway test showed significantly more suggestion effects than lows for the central viewing condition only, which may have been because the grosser overall effects in the peripheral condition suppressed these differences.

Thus, after 40 years of research on the FAE, during which it has been described as "one of the most dependable experiments for an elementary laboratory class" (Woodworth & Schlossberg, 1960, p. 424), we are confronted with evidence that the very existence of the phenomenon cannot be separated from observers' expectancies about it.

We see also, unless we assume mass psychopathy on the part of perception researchers, the ease with which the most sophisticated subjects can translate expectancies into experience without their own awareness that this is happening.

SENSORY DEPRIVATION

One blatant area of research from the standpoint of demand characteristics is the study of sensory deprivation effects. It is difficult to imagine that subjects in sensory deprivation experiments can resist behaving as such. It is quite conceivable, however, that they comply with obvious demands for some deleterious behavior in order to be cooperative or to show a normal need for stimulation, or, perhaps, because they are made vulnerable to such experiences by suggestion. The possibility exists, as well, that they try to show rich inner lives and heroic dispositions by minimizing the extent of actual effects.

Orne and Scheibe (1964) provided a convincing demonstration of motives of the first type. Subjects were recruited for hourly pay, who agreed to reserve an entire day or evening for an experiment that would last "an indefinite period of time." All were tested before and after "deprivation" on a number of measures typical of sensory deprivation studies. All spent precisely four hours in a small, quiet, amply lit room with a desk, two comfortable chairs, a stack of papers containing columns of numbers on which, they were instructed, they could perform additions as an optional activity, and a microphone for them to report their experiences.

Half the sample, however, were told they were the experimental group for a deprivation experiment and underwent the typical extraneous procedures of such studies. The experimenter wore a laboratory coat and conducted a medical interview beforehand; a tray of drugs and instruments labeled "emergency tray" was in view and subjects signed a release form which absolved the institution from responsibility for any inadvertent consequences of the experi-

Table 4. Occurrence of sensory deprivation symptoms in control and experimental subjects

Subject and group	Perceptual aberrations	Intellectual dullness	Affectively unpleasant	Anxiety fears	Spatial disorientation	Restlessness	Irritability	Total number of symptoms
Experimental								
E_1	X	X	O	O	X	O	O	3
E_2	X	O	X	X	X	X	X	6
E_3	X	X	X	O	O	X	O	4
E_4	O	X	X	X	X	X	O	5
E_5	X	X	X	X	X	X	X	7
E_6	X	X	X	X	O	X	X	6
E_7	O	X	O	O	O	O	O	1
E_8	O	O	O	O	O	O	X	1
E_9	X	X	X	X	X	X	X	7
E_{10}	X	X	O	X	X	X	X	6
Control								
C_1	O	O	O	O	O	O	O	0
C_2	X	O	O	X	O	O	O	2
C_3	O	O	O	O	O	O	O	0
C_4	O	O	O	O	O	O	O	0
C_5	X	O	X	X	X	X	O	5
C_6	O	O	O	O	O	O	O	0
C_7	X	O	O	X	O	O	X	3
C_8	O	O	O	O	O	O	X	1
C_9	O	O	O	O	O	O	O	0
C_{10}	X	X	X	X	X	X	X	7
Summary and significance								
Frequency Experimental	7	8	6	6	6	7	6	
Frequency Control	4	1	2	4	2	2	3	
Fisher exact p	.11	<.01	.06	.33	.06	<.05	.35	

Mean positive entries: Experimental group, 4.5; Control group, 1.8.
$U = 16.5$, $p < .01$, one-tailed.

Source: Orne & Scheibe (1964). Copyright © 1964 by the American Psychological Association. Reprinted by permission.

ment. There was a red pushbutton in the room labeled "emergency alarm," which they were told would obtain instant release for them if the experience became intolerable.

The balance of the sample were told they were control subjects for a sensory deprivation experiment, that they were not to undergo actual conditions of deprivation, e.g., wearing translucent goggles, white noise, restriction of activity, etc., but were simply to stay in a room alone for a period of time. Outside of the trappings described above, control and experimental subjects took part in the same experiment.

Data analyses for ten items of the test battery were comparisons of difference scores between pre- and post-tests for the two conditions. Pre-test differences between groups were not statistically significant, but analysis of covariance was used nevertheless. The remaining four items were given after the procedure only, and test scores were compared between groups.

Effects for 13 of the 14 measures were in predicted directions; four at the 5-percent level and two more at 10 percent (one-tailed tests were used throughout). Differences significant at 5 percent were: linear deviation on a spatial orientation task in which subjects drew a figure in response to directions without benefit of vision, tracing speed, distortions in the perception of simple forms, and directional shifts on the Archimedes spiral aftereffect. Differences at 10 percent were for tapping speed and logical deductions.

Deprivation-type experiences reported by subjects, both while in the room and during the postexperiment interview were coded into seven categories, and the frequencies of these for both groups are presented in Table 4. Half of the control subjects reported no symptoms at all, but none in the experimental group did so. Half of experimental subjects, but just one control subject, reported symptoms in six or all seven categories.

Of course, it is possible that subjects in the control group responded to demands to withhold such reports, but it does not seem that sitting in a comfortable room for four hours with nothing much to do should create sensory deprivation symptoms in the absence of a context to inspire these. Orne and Scheibe's description of the typical behaviors of both groups while in the room shows the process by which experimental subjects came to believe they were having aberrant experiences.

The control group subject typically started his isolation period by inspecting the room, looking through the drawers in the desk, then settling in one of the chairs, and beginning to add the numbers. After this, the pattern of activity would generally consist of long periods of repose interspersed with moderate amounts of activity on the serial additions. These subjects gave the impression, while in the chamber, of being in every way relaxed and in a pleasant frame of mind. The rate of verbalization was lower for control than for experimental subjects; typically there was but a single rather long comment at the beginning telling the experimenter how the subject intended to occupy his time while in the chamber.

In marked contrast to the repose of the controls was the general behavior of the experimental subjects. They usually began the experiment in much the same way as controls: inspection followed by some adding of numbers. But, after the first hour there would ensue a marked restlessness, a decrease in the performance of serial additions, frequent comments of displeasure at some aspect of the experience, or remarks indicating concern over lack of time sense. Occasionally experimental subjects would try to sleep, but with little success. Some exercised, while others undertook an intense and minute inspection of the room. Viewed in relation to the controls, these subjects gave an impression of almost being tortured. While the control group seemed to alternate between quiet contemplation and work with numbers, experimental subjects seemed to fluctuate between periods of unpleasant restlessness and abstract, vague periods of total inactivity. (pp. 10-11)

What do Orne and Sheibe's findings imply about the multitude of reported sensory deprivation data? It is possible that similar effects shown by subjects in "real" deprivation studies are manifestations of the treatments and not the accoutrements, but the point is that the data of those studies are of no benefit to this assumption.

SYSTEMATIC DESENSITIZATION

Systematic desensitization therapy, the innovation of Joseph Wolpe (1958), has gained more respectful attention than perhaps any other contemporary contribution of clinical psychology.

Based on classical conditioning theory and particularly the concept of reciprocal inhibition, the typical procedures of desensitization, in brief, are:

1. Determining the specific anxieties that comprise the client's problem;
2. Establishing a hierarchy of hypothetical situations or behaviors which pertain to these anxieties, which vary in aversive value for the client;
3. Training the client to keep himself relaxed during visualization of each of these situations, working stepwise up the hierarchy until the most fear-producing item is attained.

The prominence achieved by systematic desensitization testifies to the effectiveness for a variety of problems. There have been, in addition, numerous experimental demonstrations that it is desensitization and not an extraneous aspect of the therapist-client interaction that is effective (cf. Lang, 1964). These have taken the form, generally, of preselecting subjects with aversions to specific objects (e.g., spiders, snakes), using desensitization techniques with part of the sample and some control procedure, such as an analogue of another kind of therapy, with the balance, and comparing groups on a predetermined behavioral measure (e.g., handling the object).

No quibble is made here about the utility of desensitization; in fact, the author has contributed two of the case reports which support its efficacy (Geer & Silverman, 1967; Silverman & Geer, 1968). The question, however, raised in a clever study by Marcia, Rubin, and Efram (1969), concerns the experimental data which relate to the premises on which it is assumed to work.

The notion of Marcia et al. was that the precise rationale for the system given the subject or client creates a level of expectancy for improvement which may be adequte to explain results, particularly inasmuch as the subject/client is told each time he completes a hierarchy item that he is closer to cure.

They conducted a typical desensitization experiment, using subjects who stated they were very much afraid of spiders or snakes and approach distances to preserved specimens of these as the criterion behavior. One comparison group, however, was administered a procedure called "T-Scope Therapy," which was somewhat antithetical in principle to desensitization, but was given a rationale sounding equally rigorous and plausible. These subjects received mildly painful electric shocks during exposure of what they thought were subliminal presentations of fear-related stimuli. Subjects were shown polygraphic records (also contrived) after each session indicating that they were gradually decreasing in anxiety to the stimuli.

An additional group (low expectancy T-scope) were told they were in a control condition and that the slides were empty, and received no feedback about their autonomic responses. Finally, there were control conditions in which subjects were simply tested before and after intervals equivalent to the treatment times.

In terms of differences in approach distances to the feared objects before and after treatments, the means of desensitization and high expectancy T-scope groups were similar and both improved significantly more than either low expectancy T-scope or no-treatment subjects. Proportions of subjects showing improvement were: .83 for high expectancy T-scope; .78 for desensitization; .43 for low expectancy T-scope, and .17 for no-treatment controls. (The only significant differences were between no-treatment controls and both high expectancy T-scope and desensitization.) Improvement data for high expectancy T-scope and desensitization groups were compared to those of two prior reported studies of desensitization effectiveness (Lang, 1964; Lang, Lazovik, & Reynolds, 1965), which used a similar desensitization paradigm, and were found to be equal or superior for all comparisons.

Thus, it appears that in the psychological experiment electric shock is as effective as systematic desensitization for reducing anxieties, as long as expectancies and feedback about improvement are constant.

Were these fears actually dispelled by conformity to the experimenter-therapists' suggestion? An alternate possibility was suggested by an experience of the author in attempting pilot work for a study based on much the same premises as Marcia et al.

I solicited female subjects from one of my classes by asking for those "who did not think they could handle a preserved tarantula spider." Ten of 12 in the class volunteered; six were selected at random and tested. None would lift or even touch the spider initially, though some did after the procedures of the pilot study.

Before moving to the experiment proper, however, I became concerned that my method of solicitation may have conveyed to subjects a demand *not* to handle the spider. Hence, I asked for female volunteers for "an interesting experiment," and, as the girls appeared I told each to "go to the table, pick up the preserved tarantula that you see there with one hand, and place it in the other." After the first ten complied, showing mild hesitation at the most, I suspended further attempts to do the study as planned.

It is reasonable to assume that subjects in Marcia et al.'s experiment and other desensitization studies could have, as well, performed the fear-provoking behaviors *before* treatments *if they perceived that the experimenter expected them to.* And it remains to be shown that desensitization experiments have any application to the therapy in practice where anxieties have been tested in life rather than in psychological laboratories.

4

Role-Related Motives and Psychological Data: Voluntary Behavior

For the reader who, at this point, is impressed by the scope and pervasiveness of artifact in psychological research, the present section may be gilding the lily. Here we discuss areas of research in which the responses which represent the dependent variables are considered to be voluntarily given, and the influences of role-related motives are generally less subtle than in studies we have previously described.

ATTITUDE CHANGE

This prominent area of social psychology is a prime example. Subjects in attitude-change studies are usually presented with persuasive communications followed by opinion questions based on their contents and, despite the occasional attempts to distract them from the apparent purpose of these procedures or statements reminding them that there are no "right" or "wrong" opinions, it does not require a superior intellect to realize that persuasibility is being scrutinized. The questions, then, that must obsess the subject and guide his responses to a significant extent are: "Does this experimenter expect me to be persuaded?" and "Why?"

Further, these studies almost always use topics which are not particularly salient for subjects in order to provide latitude for influence. Thus, even the rare bird who works to overcome considerations of self-presentation and answer honestly could probably not divine *what his opinions* were in the absence of the experimental contrivances.

The variability of responses in attitude-change studies can be plausibly attributed to the fact that persuasion has negative and positive connotations. It may become associated in subjects' minds with non-critical conformity and over-dependence, or with open-mindedness and flexibility. In a brief, unpublished study, Arthur Shulman and I presented subjects with a standard-type attitude-change measure, containing a typical introductory statement, messages, and opinion items, varying only the designation of the research sponsor listed on the face sheet as "Institute for the Study of Propaganda Effects" or the "Institute for the Study of Communication and Information Processing," and found dramatic and highly significant differences in attitude scores.

Given that subject's dilemmas about the meanings of their responses are relatively straightforward, attitude studies are prototypic for the study of role-related behavior. Silverman and Shulman (1970), in fact, have presented and documented five propositions about sources of artifact in attitude research which encompass most of the concepts discussed in previous chapters.

First, they proposed that in the absence of specific demand characteristics in the experiment for opinion change or non-change, subjects will tend to show change. This is based on the notion that subjects will assume that an experimenter who has taken the trouble of constructing persuasive attempts expects people to be at least somewhat persuaded, and to respond otherwise would probably be abnormal.

Silverman (1968a) performed the following test of this contention: A female research assistant appeared in 25 psychology classes, comprising multiple sections of four courses. In ten of these, she was introduced by the instructors as "Dr. Silverman's research assistant," and she asked for a few minutes of the students' time to conduct "a short experiment." In another ten, she was introduced as a representative of a campus student group, and she indicated that she was soliciting reactions to a report the group had prepared. In both conditions she distributed the same communication, advocating the use of closed-circuit television for large lecture classes, followed by four opinion items on the issue. The remaining five classes comprised the baseline group and were given the items without the message. Here the experimenter was introduced as someone from the psychology department who was doing a brief survey.

All subjects recorded their sexes on the forms, and half the classes in each of the two experimental conditions were asked to include their names as well. Sections of the four courses were counterbalanced as evenly as possible across conditions.

Both groups who had been given the communication showed more positive attitudes toward televised lectures than baseline subjects, but subjects who were told they were in an experiment showed more influence of the message than those who were not, ($p<.01$), and this effect of context was greater for females than for males ($p<.09$) and for non-anonymous subjects than for those who were anonymous, ($p<.05$).

The second and third propositions of Silverman and Shulman dealt directly with the relationships between demand characteristics and evaluation apprehension discussed in Chapter 2. They stated that: subjects will tend to comply with specific cues regarding the experimenter's expectations, whether these involve compliance with or resistance to attitude-change attempts, unless subjects perceive a specific response to be associated with favorable self-presentation, in which case they will make this response whether it is consistent or inconsistent with demand characteristics.

Evidence for the first conjecture comes from studies based on the frequently cited demonstrations by Staats and Staats (1957, 1958) that attitudes, defined broadly as positive or negative dispositions toward any object or symbol, can be classically conditioned. Staats and Staats' procedure was to visually present a list of six nonsense syllables to subjects, repeatedly, each followed by a spoken word from a larger list, allegedly as a memory experiment. Spoken words with positive or negative connotations (e.g., beautiful, healthy, ugly, sick) were systematically associated with some syllables, and subjects then rated all syllables on scales of "pleasant-unpleasant."

Probably, as most psychologists, this writer is not skeptical that attitudes are sometimes classically conditioned. I am skeptical, however, despite Staats and Staats' data, that an experimenter speaking the word "beautiful" is a sufficient CS to evoke the same kind of response to a nonsense syllable or anything else as when a man is attracted to a woman who looks like his mother or to a hat similar to one that was worn by a dear friend.

As in the earliest verbal conditioning studies, Staats and Staats asked subjects briefly what they thought about the purpose of the experiment and excluded the few who were aware. Similar to the later verbal conditioning studies, however, replications of Staats and Staats by Cohen (1964), Insko and Oakes (1966), and M.M. Page (1969), using more stringent questioning procedures, found that many more subjects were aware and that "conditioning" occurred only with these. Insko and Oakes made the qualification that conditioning was found with subjects who professed awareness of the nature of the associations but not the experimental hypothesis, though it seems a discredit to human intelligence to believe that subjects realized that positive or negative words were repeatedly being spoken after specific syllables but did not suspect that they were expected to rate these syllables accordingly on a scale of affective value. These authors reported, also, a phenomenon rarely, if ever, seen in conditioning research, a complete absence of extinction on later trials without the CS, though we may not share their expressed puzzlement about this. Subjects were aware that the CS had ended, but they probably were not sure what they were supposed to do about it.

M.M. Page (1969), using more direct questions to assess awareness of the hypothesis, found conditioning only in subjects aware of both associations and expectations. He found, also, that conditioning and awareness were significantly higher in subjects seen later in the semester of their introductory psychology course.

A. Staats (1969) posed the alternative explanation for all of these findings that subjects were probably made aware of associations and expectations by being forced to think about them during the extended postexperiment interviews. This is possible, but it would be a parsimonious alternative only if we could assume that subjects generally tried to be honest about their motives during experiments on brief or extended postexperimental interviews. The data described in Chapter 2 by Levy (1967), Golding and Lichtenstein (1970), White and Shumsky (1972), and Newberry (1973), however, clearly suggest the converse.

Studies by Rosnow and Rosenthal (1966) and Rosnow (1968) provide further evidence of the operation of demand characteristics in attitude research. In the first of these, students who volunteered to be subjects and students who were induced by a course requirement were given communications either for or against college fraternities. Pre-measures of subjects' opinions were taken earlier in a different context. Volunteers changed their opinions less than non-volunteers in the direction of the pro-fraternity message, but more in the direction of the anti-fraternity message. In a test of comparable subjects, it was discovered that the faculty member conducting the research was generally considered to be opposed to fraternities; thus, the conclusion of Rosnow and Rosenthal was that volunteers, being more compliant with demands, were more responsive to the message when they perceived that it represented the position of the communicator.

In a second study, Rosnow (1968) presented passages comprised of pro- or anti-fraternity arguments either singly to separate groups of subjects or together, combined in both orders. Subjects in the one-sided conditions changed attitudes in the appropriate directions, but in both two-sided conditions there was significant change toward the anti-fraternity position. Rosnow's conclusion was that in the absence of specific cues about the expected direction of change, subjects moved toward the attitude they attributed to the experimenter.

Silverman and Regula (1968) provided evidence that attitude-change subjects respond in the direction of favorable self-presentation when such a response is made apparent, despite their percepts of the experimenters' expectations. Their study was based on Festinger and Maccoby's (1964) successful test of the hypothesis that distraction during a persuasive attempt increases influence by "inhibiting counterarguing." Festinger and Maccoby exposed subjects to a recorded persuasive message and the visual track of an irrelevant film simultaneously. Inasmuch as no explanation was given for this procedure, Silverman and Regula reasoned that subjects surmised that the experimenters were trying to impair their abilities to concentrate, and were thus motivated to show that they had attended well enough to the message to be persuaded. Silverman and Regula introduced static into a recorded persuasive communication; but in one condition they explained that it was caused by an error in transcribing the talk from a radio broadcast; in another, they said that it was part of the experiment. Both of these groups were compared to a control group, who heard a clear tape, and were asked, after the experiment proper, what they thought about the purpose of the static.

There were significantly greater persuasibility scores with distraction *only* for subjects who were *not* told that the static was inadvertent and who indicated that its purpose was to interfere with or test their concentration. The balance of subjects in the "intentional" distraction condition were significantly *less* persuaded than the control group, but the rather sophisticated hypotheses attributed to the experimenter by a majority of these showed clearly that they had responded to demands that would lead to non-persuasion (e.g., the experimenter expected the effects of the frustration of the static to generalize to the speaker, or he expected the message would be partially comprehended and thus interpreted in line with their original opinions). The data of the group who had been told the static was accidental were indistinguishable from the controls.

Proposition Four described some of the circumstances in which subjects might tend to deliberately respond counter to demand characteristics; for example when they are frustrated as an intentional or incidental part of the experiment. Based on this reasoning, Silverman and Kleinman (1967) offered an alternative interpretation for the data of several studies showing that experimentally induced frustration increased minority-group prejudice, (e.g., Cowen, Landes, & Schaet, 1959; Stricker, 1963). Their contention was that frustrated subjects may vent anger by attempting to "spoil" the experiment, which may take the form of expressing attitudes, like minority-group prejudice, which they perceive the experimenter would not expect in the fair-minded, intellectual climate of a university.

Silverman and Kleinman followed a procedure typical of frustration-prejudice experiments. A group of female college subjects were given several problem-solving tasks, with less time allowed than is normally needed, and were deprecated by the experimenter for their performances. Then a semantic differential-type attitude scale (Osgood, Suci, & Tannenbaum, 1957) was distributed on the pretense that these data were needed for another project. A control group received the attitude scales only.

The attitude scale contained two concepts related to prejudice and four others designed to measure "deviant" responding. These were: *cheating on examinations, sexual promiscuity; the value of education;* and *democratic forms of government.*

Frustrated subjects showed significantly more prejudice than controls, but were also significantly more positive toward cheating on examinations and sexual promiscuity and negative toward the value of education and democratic forms of government. Further, the correlation coefficient between prejudice scores and scores indicating deviant responses on the other scales combined reached the rare (for psychological research) magnitude of .86 for frustrated subjects, but was of zero-order for controls.

Another set of studies showing effects of frustration (Silverman

& Shulman, 1969) was based on demonstrations by Janis, Kaye, and Kirschner (1965) and Dabbs and Janis (1965) that "eating-while-reading" a persuasive message increases its positive effect. Similar to Staats and Staats (1957, 1958), Janis and his colleagues made their predictions from classical conditioning theory, contending that the positive responses elicited by eating would become generalized to the communications. Dabbs and Janis had also taken into account the possibility that the refreshments served by the experimenter might have disposed subjects to comply more with demand characteristics, by showing that a control group who were served before rather than during the messages were not affected. The puzzling aspects of Dabbs and Janis' data, however, were that eating-while-reading increased persuasion only when the experimenter had previously expressed agreement with the messages; when he had expressed disagreement, eating-while-reading *decreased* persuasion. Dabbs and Janis considered their conditioning hypothesis "partially supported," but Silverman and Shulman interpreted their data as suggesting that, for some odd reason, refreshments served during the messages, but not beforehand, were associated with greater compliance with specific demands both for persuasion and non-persuasion.

In pondering this paradox, Silverman and Shulman noted that both studies were intentionally conducted during hours when subjects would be expected to be hungry. They conjectured that the frustration of being kept from meals by an experiment might have made subjects generally non-responsive or antagonistic toward demands, an effect which would have been attenuated in the groups that were served during the reading sessions, but not in the groups that were served beforehand, inasmuch as the light refreshments that were given them and then withdrawn may have aggravated rather than appeased hunger-frustration.

A negative relationship approaching significance ($p<.15$) was found by Silverman and Shulman between hunger, assessed by asking subjects after the study when they had last taken any food, and persuasion, measured by a standard opinion-change instrument, for females only. Again, for females only, both hunger and persuasion were negatively related to an independent measure of compliance with demand characteristics[1] (at $p<.01$ and $p<.15$, respectively).

[1] Livant (1963) reported that words with two grammatical forms (e.g., dream) were rated as more active on a semantic differential when they were presented as verbs than as nouns. Cataldo, Silverman and Brown (1967) discovered that these differences occurred only when subjects could compare their verb and noun ratings, and they attributed Livant's effects to demand characteristics. An adaptation of Livant's scale was used in this and an additional study reported later in the text as a measure of tendencies to comply with demands.

In a following study, experimenters voiced either agreement or disagreement with the persuasive messages in the manner of Dabbs and Janis, and hunger was measured by time since last food intake and by subjects' reports of how hungry they felt. Once again, there were no differences for males, but female hungry subjects showed *less* of the opinion changes advocated by the messages when the experimenter agreed and *more* when he disagreed, than their non-hungry counterparts. (Significance levels for these interactions were p<.06, for the self-report and p<.15 for the time measures.)

Why did females and not males show these effects? The only clue we have are the findings of Silverman (1968a), described earlier, that females, more so than males, responded to an attitude-change measure in terms of demand characteristics. At any rate, it appears that we ought to know how hungry our subjects are in addition to everything else that can affect the ways they decide to bounce.

We noted earlier the contention by Orne (1962) that when demands are very explicit, subjects often deliberately respond in a negative manner. Illustration of this principle in attitude-change research comes from a review by Lana (1969) of more than a dozen studies on the effects of "pre-testing"; that is, administering attitude scales before and after persuasive attempts rather than afterward only. Whenever there were differences between these procedures, measured by comparisons of post-test attitudes, they consistently showed a *dampening* of opinion change in the pre-test conditions.

These differences might reflect the effects of prior public commitment rather than negative responding, but Rosnow and Suls (1969) discovered an interesting interaction, accountable by the latter notion only. In their studies, reduction of opinion-change with pre-tests occurred for non-volunteer subjects only; while pre-testing *facilitated* persuasion for volunteers.

A further example of obstinacy when demands are "too obvious" was provided by Brehm and Krasin (cf. Brehm, 1966, pp. 106-108). Subjects were given an opinion questionnaire, then were shown contrived answers to the same items (allegedly from peers), then were retested. There were significant changes in the directions of the peers' opinions, directly related to the magnitude of discrepancy, *except* when the experimenter mentioned that he expected them to be influenced. Here, the effect was completely reversed; change was in the *opposite* direction from the peers' opinions and directly related to discrepancy.

The final proposition of Silverman and Shulman stated that in studies relating some individual difference variable to attitude change, spurious results will be obtained to the extent that the individual difference variable relates to role-related behavior. As we discussed in regard to verbal conditioning research, this may occur because the individual difference variable is genuinely associated with tendencies toward compliance with demands or favorable self-presentation, or because the measure of the variable, as well as the measure of attitude-change, is responded to in terms of these motives.

For example, Sherman (1967) questioned the relationship, reported by Katz, Sarnoff, and McClintock (1956) and McClintock (1958), between "other-directedness" and responsiveness to authoritarian-type persuasive appeals; that is, appeals based on conformity to others' opinions. She felt that the experimenters' introductory comments for these arguments contained a variety of implicit demands for attitude change, and she found that the other-directedness-persuasion relationship occurred only with the original introduction and was, in fact, *reversed* when an introduction containing implicit demands for resistance was substituted.

Finally, we must question the veracity of what one text-writer (Middlebrook, 1974, p. 190) has called "one of the most consistent findings in laboratory studies" that females are more persuasible, in general, than males. Though several studies have supported this cliché (e.g., Janis & Field, 1959; Silverman, Ford, & Morganti, 1966), one experiment described earlier in this section (Silverman, 1968a) suggested that this sex difference emerged only when persuasibility was tested in the context of an experiment. The data showed, in fact, that when the same message was presented in a "life" context, females were significantly *less* persuaded than males.

It seems likely that the self-presentation of the male in psychological experiments is associated more with resistance to influence, and females are more willing to show susceptibility, if this is what the experimenter seems to want. Silverman, Ford, and Morganti (1966) found that favorable self-presentation, as measured by social desirability scales, was negatively related to persuasibility for males only. In a study described in the following section, Stricker, Messick, and Jackson (1967) observed that males, but not females, scoring high on social desirability scales were more apt to report suspiciousness of conformity-testing procedures, with suspiciousness inversely related to conformity.

These separate constellations of male and female role-behaviors in influence experiments may be of limited interest in their own right, but they clearly obviate any attempt to generalize sex differences from these studies to behavior outside of the psychological laboratory.

It is apparent from all of the above that there is a vast amount of variance in attitude-change measures that can be attributed to role-related behavior, and it is not surprising that studies in this area that generate sufficient interest to be repeated are frequently not replicated or turn out in opposite directions; for example, the primacy-recency effect (Lana, 1964), the effects of reward for attitude-discrepant behavior (Abelson, Aronson, McGuire, Newcomb, Rosenberg, & Tannenbaum, 1968, pp. 801-33), or the relationship of personality to persuasibility (McGuire, 1966). From the thoughtfulness of the theories that spawned these studies, we would expect the data to be at least moderately generalizable, but different experimental situations can easily produce differences in the assumptions subjects make about the meanings of their behaviors, and their dispositions, based on these assumptions, to respond one way or another. It is not surprising, either, that in the few instances where investigators have studied the relationship of attitude-change scores obtained in an experiment to behavior outside of the experiment it has been virtually nil (Festinger, 1964).

CONFORMITY

This, also, has been a central topic in social psychology. Though seemingly synonymous with attitude change, the distinction is that conformity behavior is considered to represent sheer imitation of others whereas attitude change may involve reorganizations of beliefs and opinions in response to new information. The methodological problems for the two, however, are very much similar.

Most discussions of conformity research begin with homage to the classic experiments of Asch (1956) in which subjects, seen in groups for an alleged perception test, were asked to select one of three lines which most closely approximated a standard line in length. There was one obvious correct answer, but there was just one actual subject per group. The others, confederates of the experimenter, were all seated so that they responded prior to the subject and all gave the same incorrect answer. Asch was impressed by the number of conforming responses in this situation, generally a majority of subjects, but he was not oblivious to the fact that ". . . it crossed the minds of many . . . that the majority might be deliberately misleading. . . ." (Asch, 1956, p. 29).

Rather than developing methods to study conformity where subjects' minds might not be crossed in this manner, social psychologists embarked on a multitude of experiments using various mechanized forms of the Asch paradigm (e.g., Crutchfield, 1955; Olmstead & Blake, 1955), which probably served to increase the unreality of subjects' experiences. In these, the subject sat by himself in a cubicle, rather than at the end of a row of other subjects, and observed flashing lights which ostensibly signaled the answers of others who, he was told, were sitting in other cubicles. Thus, he could not believe if he wanted to that the experimenter was truly interested in perception and had, perhaps, been shortsighted for the sake of expedience in allowing subjects to hear each others' responses. Nevertheless, conformity apparatuses became almost standard equipment in departments of psychology—social psychology's answer to the operant conditioning laboratory.

It should not surprise us at this point that studies using these methods, typically with university students, found rates of suspiciousness on postexperimental questionnaires hovering about the same 5-percent mark as the early verbal conditioning studies (e.g., Crutchfield, 1955; Linde & Patterson, 1964; Vaughan, 1964). Was this true ignorance or another instance of subject contriteness? The question, at least to this writer, seemed resolved by the findings of Stricker, Messick, and Jackson (1967) that when more guileless subjects, high school students, were used, accurate postexperimental reports of the purpose of the procedure increased to 48 percent.

Admissions of suspiciousness were correlated with performance as well, although in a direction opposite that for verbal conditioning and classical conditioning of attitudes. Suspicious subjects conformed less (or subjects who conformed less admitted suspiciousness), which may be a function, also, of the different categories of subjects in these studies. A high school student who detects deception and resists demands may be proud to report this, whereas the more socialized university psychology student may be nervous about one-upping the experimenter. On the other hand, it may simply be that reporting an incorrect perception in response to group pressure evokes more evaluation apprehension than the type of conformity elicited in the verbal or classical conditioning experiments.

Schulman (1967) administered a mechanized Asch-type procedure under conditions in which subjects were led to believe either that the experimenter would or would not be aware of their individual responses. The conformity of males decreased significantly in the former condition—females did not, as we might expect from the discussion of the previous section, and, in fact, showed a moderate but non-significant increase.

AGGRESSION

Social psychologists have given continuous concern to the relevance (or non-relevance) of their findings for social problems. Silverman (1971) has suggested that the reason for the lack of impact of social psychology upon society is not because we have been engaged in non-relevant topics, but because the data we produce are generally not relevant to the constructs to which they pertain. "If we do not acquire the insights to generate social psychological data that are veridical to behavior outside of the specific research paradigms from which they were spawned, we will find that it is just as easy to proliferate pseudo-knowledge about social problems as anything else" (Silverman, 1971, p. 584).

A case in point are the experiments of Berkowitz and LePage (1967) on the effects of aggression-related stimuli, specifically guns, on aggressive behavior. The subject in these studies was informed that the investigators were interested in effects of stress. He was required to write an answer to a problem given him and exchange answers with another subject, actually a confederate, with the instruction that each would then evaluate the other by giving him one to ten electric shocks from another room. It was contrived that the actual subject responded last and he received either one or seven shocks from his partner.

The critical variable in these experiments was the presence of a pair of guns, placed casually near the shock apparatus, and explained as having been left in the laboratory by someone else for some other experiment. The presence of the weapons, as well as the number of shocks received, increased the number of shocks the subject returned, and Berkowitz (1968) was led to the dramatic conclusion that "The finger pulls the trigger, but the trigger may be also pulling the finger." It was an important scientific statement from the standpoint of legislation regarding private ownership of weapons, as well as for a theory about aggressive behavior.

As so many others, Berkowitz and LePage (1967) assessed their subjects' suspicions with one general question and excluded the few who expressed awareness of the deceptions. Page and Scheidt (1971), however, attempted several replications of this study with a more elaborate postexperimental questionnaire, and found considerably higher suspicion rates. They found also that the "weapons effect" was "elusive," and seemed to occur in relation to the sophistication of subjects about psychological research. Specifically:

1. "Naive" subjects, introductory psychology students who were participating in their first experiment, showed low rates of reported suspicion and *no weapons effect.*
2. "Slightly sophisticated" subjects, those who had participated in one other study involving deception, showed high rates of reported suspicion and the *weapons effect.*
3. "Highly sophisticated" subjects, those who had completed the introductory course with its multiple participation requirement and were currently enrolled in a social psychology course, showed high rates of reported suspicion and a *significant reversal of the weapons effect.*

There are several apparent hypotheses we might invoke at this point for why the nature of the game for subjects changed as their experience with psychological research increased, but about one matter there is little speculation—that a game it was.

EXPECTANCY DISCONFIRMATION

Nearly 50 years ago, Tinklepaugh (1928) demonstrated that if a hungry monkey is given the expectancy that he is going to eat a banana, he will refuse to eat a lettuce leaf. This was probably no surprise to anyone who has tried to feed cereal to a pet dog with the odor of fresh meat present, but it probably represents the earliest systematic demonstration of the motivational properties of expectancy disconfirmation.

Aronson, Carlsmith, and Darley (1963) put the properties of expectancy disconfirmation to a sterner test in some research with people subjects. They hypothesized that a person who is led to expect a mildly unpleasant event, if given a choice, may prefer to endure the event than not in order to avoid "dissonance" (Festinger, 1957) associated with the mental preparations he had made. Subjects were given a series of trials in both a weight discrimination task, which was considered to be effectively neutral, and an unpleasant bitterness discrimination task, and were told that they would have to repeat either one or the other. Prior to the second series, however, the experimenter pretended that he had been in error in making the assignment and offered the subject his choice, indicating that it made absolutely no difference which task he repeated. No one in the weight task expectancy condition chose the taste task but a significant proportion of taste task expectancy subjects did so.

Goldberg (1965) suggested that these subjects may have anticipated the experimental hypothesis and responded accordingly, and he attempted to vary demands by inserting a confederate subject who made one or the other choice prior to the real subject. In addition, he had conditions similar to Aronsen et al. The only subjects in this study who chose the taste task were from the group with the taste expectancy who heard the confederate make this choice also, a result which did not fully substantiate the demand characteristics interpretation, but cast some doubt as to whether dissonance reduction was the mediator.

Silverman (1968b) offered another interpretation of subject motives in this situation. He considered that subjects may not have been complying with demands, per se, but may have been moved to select the unpleasant task in order not to indicate to the experimenter their displeasure with his original assignment. This would suggest that the personage of the experimenter could easily effect responses, and may explain Goldberg's failure to replicate in the no-confederate conditions. Glenda Denham and I, in an unpublished set of studies, varied status and measured "likability" of experimenters to ascertain whether these factors, which we thought would influence subjects' desires not to displease, would relate to expectancy disconfirmation effects. They did not, though we did find *significant differences in the effect among our eight experimenters* and concluded that some aspect of the experimenter-subject relationship accounts for choices of the unpleasant task.

REPRESSERS AND SENSITIZERS

These constructs refer to contrasting modes of ego-defense which are assumed to characterize individuals. The represser tends to repress threatening events or impulses; the sensitizer uses defense mechanisms which provide some expression or recognition of the source of threat. For example, a represser would tend to inhibit feelings of hostility; a sensitizer may sublimate or rationalize about them.

There are several widely used scales for measuring repression-sensitization (Byrne, 1964), and one consistent finding is that people who score high on sensitization tend to show more anxiety than repressers on self-report-type tests and less on indirect tests, such as autonomic responsiveness (Joy, 1963; Ullman & McReynolds, 1963; Lazarus & Alfert, 1964; Lomont, 1965). These differences are congruent to the theory of repression-sensitization; sensitizers would be expected both to recognize sources of anxiety and discharge tension from these more than repressers.

Lefcourt (1966), however, was intrigued by an alternative possibility: that repression-sensitization scores, and differences between these types on anxiety measures, reflected different concepts by subjects about the meanings of their responses. He asked two questions of subjects who had completed Byrne's (1961) repression-sensitization scale: "What do you believe this test measures?" and "Describe the sort of person who would fill out the questionnaire in exactly the opposite manner that you did." He found, with very few exceptions, that repressers believed the test was concerned with mental illness. The great majority of sensitizers, on the other hand, perceived the test as a measure of "emotionality" or "honesty with one's self." Whereas repressers felt that people answering in the opposite direction would be "abnormal" or "ill," sensitizers thought that opposite-responders were "liars" or "not too bright."

In a second study, Lefcourt administered the Thematic Apperception Test to both types with instructions either that the experiment concerned "creative imagination" or that the investigator was "collecting norms for contrast with the performance of mentally ill populations." The "affect-ideations," or emotional contents, of sensitizers' stories were significantly higher than repressers' in the creative imagination condition, but were significantly and dramatically reduced under the mental illness instruction. "Sensitizors . . . who usually perceive emotional expressions more positively were expected and found to write in emotional terms more frequently than repressors. However, when the situation was structured as involving an evaluation of mental illness, sensitizors became less expressive, closely resembling the repressors who customarily equate emotionality with abnormality" (p. 447).

Thus, we may readily conclude that sensitizers express more anxiety in psychological studies in response to direct questions, because they believe that it reflects a favorable trait. Why do repressers show more anxiety on indirect tests? It may be simply that these subjects, who tend to equate psychological measures with mental illness, are made more anxious by these tests.

SOME OTHER "DEEP" PERSONALITY TRAITS

Lefcourt's analysis demonstrated that the traits revealed by subjects on personality tests may be merely a reflection of how they solved the dilemma of what the psychologist was trying to measure. There is another strategy of subjects confronted with psychological inventories, however, which may be employed when the dilemma is not easily resolvable or when they simply do not care enough, and that is to say nothing about themselves. One neat way to do this is to respond to items in a stereotyped way, irrespective of their contents. The behavior of subjects so disposed seems to be to mark "agree" to everything, and the phenomenon is so prevalent in psychological testing that it has earned the label "acquiescent response set."

Acquiescent response set is generally regarded as an idiosyncracy, a minor source of artifact that can be readily relegated to non-systematic error variance by assuring that half the items in the scale are phrased so that disagreement is indicative of the trait in question. If we view it instead as a manifestation of a basic disposition in subjects' approaches to psychological measures, we may see how data becomes distorted despite our attempts at control.

Peabody (1961) selected items from well-known scales measuring authoritarianism, anti-Semitism, dogmatism, and conservatism in which all items were phrased in the direction whereby agreement represented the trait. He wrote counterparts for these items, phrased in the opposite direction, and constructed two forms of each test, each with half the items in one and half in the other direction. Subjects were administered both forms, from two to four weeks apart.

The percentages of responses which were "double-agreement," that is, cases in which both forms of a given item were agreed to, were 33, 32, 19, and 21, respectively, for the four scales. If we add to these the cases of "double-disagreement," then the total percentages of instances in which items were answered with disregard for content were 43, 39, 28, and 30 respectively. Peabody found also that for the authoritarian, anti-Semitism, and dogmatism scales, the great majority of responses which were logically consistent, that is, the subject disagreed where he had previously agreed or the converse, were in the direction indicating a lack of the trait. An analysis of the 163 individual subjects in terms of most frequent response-combination—double-agreement, double-disagreement, consistent pro-trait or consistent anti-trait—revealed one authoritarian, two dogmatists, and seven anti-Semites.

Then what do we know about the people who are classified according to the various "isms" that seem to preoccupy personality theorists? Are the good guys, the non-authoritarians, non-dogmatists, etc., subjects who deny negatively toned traits on psychological tests? Do those who score at the other end of the distribution actually possess some moderate amount of the characteristic, or do they earn their position on the continuum by responding in some stereotyped way to everything? One conclusion seems as valid as another. Other interpretations have been given for Peabody's data (Rokeach, 1963; Samelson, 1964), which Peabody (1966) has answered, but this rhetoric offers little. We are still left with the fact that we are labeling subjects authoritarian or ethnocentric or dogmatic who are checking our items in an extremely casual manner and quite independent of content. Nor do the data of studies using these inventories provide encouragement for construct validity. As in so many areas of behavioral research, they are inconsistent (e.g., Budner, 1960; Johnson, Tovcivia, & Poprick, 1968; Larsen, 1969; Zipple & Norman, 1966), and we may now be convinced that the nature of subjects' motives in psychological experiments and the factors that influence these are such that anyone can support any theory with any set of measures if he works at it long enough.

5

Other Mediators of Role-Related Behavior

The prior two chapters have mainly illustrated the ways by which role-related subject motives interact with experimental strategies to produce artifact. We have introduced at times factors which are external to the research design proper which contribute also to the processes by which role-related motives become manifest in data: e.g., sophistication of subjects, their volunteer versus non-volunteer status, experimenter expectancies. The present chapter comprises a more detailed discussion of some of these factors.

VOLUNTEERS AND NON-VOLUNTEERS

Interest in differences between volunteers and non-volunteers in psychological research dates back more than two decades (e.g., Maslow & Sakoda, 1952; Cochran, Mosteller, & Tukey, 1953; Locke, 1954). Rosenthal (1965) and Rosnow and Rosenthal (1969, 1970) have made extensive reviews of this literature, with the general conclusions that volunteers tend to be more intelligent, better educated, higher in need for approval, more sociable, more arousal-seeking, less conventional, less authoritarian, more often first-born, and younger than non-volunteers. Silverman and Margulis (1973) have explored another dimension of volunteer effects, showing that when members of an introductory psychology subject-pool are allowed to choose between participation in a study related to their "personalities" and one of more benign content, volunteers for the former were apt to be more autonomous, complexity-seeking, extroverted, skeptical of conventional religious beliefs, diverse in intellectual pursuits, and less practical in general outlook.

Rosnow and Rosenthal pointed out limitations for the generalization of data based on studies using volunteers or non-volunteers exclusively, but Kruglanski (1973) offered a disclaimer. She suggested that volunteer, non-volunteer differences, as all questions of subject representativeness, are critical in survey research or some other endeavor where "*accuracy* in estimating a given population parameter is most desirable. By contrast, in experimental research, the prime objective is to demonstrate the effects of experimental treatments upon a given phenomenon of interest . . . the intended inference is not to a unique aggregate of individuals (or a specific population) but to man in general or even organisms in general. Consequently, the emphasis is on what is *common* to all men, or all organisms. . . ." (pp.352-353). On this basis, she argued that selecting a sample to represent a broad population, which enhances variability among subjects, may not be at all desirable inasmuch as it may serve to suppress experimental effects by producing inflated error terms. She thus concluded that the methodological importance of volunteer, non-volunteer differences had been exaggerated.

We share a separate concern with Rosnow and Rosenthal, however, which is not based on the issue of the generalizability of *valid* data obtained with a limited sample. Our interest is whether there are aspects of role behavior which distinguish volunteers and non-volunteers, which can account for differences in the effects of experimental treatments, and thus increase our perspectives about sources of *invalidity* in psychological research. Studies by Rosnow and Rosenthal (1966) and Rosnow and Suls (1970), described in the previous chapter, provide illustration. They showed that the effects of various treatments used by attitude-change researchers were *opposite* for volunteers and non-volunteers, based on the supposed greater tendencies of the former to comply with demand characteristics.

Horowitz (1969) has provided an additional example, based on a classic attitude experiment by Janis and Feshbach (1953). By an artful juxtaposition of conditioning and analytic theory, Janis and Feshbach formulated a hypothesis to flaunt conventional wisdom, that persuasive appeals which arouse high anxiety about not conforming to the dictates of the message are *less* effective than those which arouse low anxiety. Their conformation of this hypothesis with high and low fear appeals about dental hygiene was sufficiently compelling to generate a series of replication attempts, and these, as we might by now expect, demonstrated positive relationships between fear arousal and attitude change about as frequently as the original negative. In perusing this literature, Horowitz noted that negative relationships seemed to occur with non-volunteer samples and· positive relationships with volunteers, and he confirmed these observations using two levels of fear arousal about drug abuse.

In a following study, Horowitz and Gumenik (1970) confronted the question of whether the dispositions of subjects which underlie these diverse effects were related to personality differences of volunteers and non-volunteers, or to the act of volunteering. Using a technique borrowed from Rosnow and Rosenthal (1966), they asked for volunteers for a fictitious experiment which was then canceled, and later recruited, as part of a course requirement, those subjects who had and had not volunteered. In addition, half the subjects in each of these groups were given the *impression* of volition by being allowed a choice of studies to participate in. (The critical study was made to seem more attractive.) A positive fear arousal attitude-change relationship was found in the volunteer group, regardless of choice condition. Non-volunteers *who were allowed choice* showed the same, but *non-volunteers* who were *not* allowed choice showed a negative relationship. Thus, both internal and external factors related to volunteering were instrumental.

We are left with a typical dilemma. Do we accept the data of non-volunteers as support for Janis and Feshbach's theory and assume that volunteers in the high fear conditions were deceived in their attempt to comply with demand characteristics by the counter-intuitional nature of the hypothesis? Or do we assume that volunteers provided veridical data, while non-volunteers perversely responded to high fear attempts by non-acceptance of the message. Most likely, *no one* was very much motivated by fear arousal; all were far too busy deciding what to do about the experimenter's obvious attempt to frighten them into agreement, and volunteers tended to comply while non-volunteers did the opposite. In any case, we know as much on empirical grounds about fear arousal and attitude change as we did before the Janis and Feshbach study.

For our final case in point, we return to the "Zeigarnik Effect" (greater recall of uncompleted versus completed tasks) which, as noted in Chapter 1, was one of the potential examples of "extraneous subject motivation" given by Rosenzweig in 1933. Some 36 years after Zeigarnik's (1927) paper, Green (1963) showed that the effect was only obtained with volunteer subjects. Non-volunteers showed a *reversal*. (All of the early research replicating the phenomenon was done before the heyday of subject pools, solely with volunteers [cf. Kruglanski, 1973].) Then, what were Gestalt psychologists measuring in all of those studies? If it was "need for closure," could it be that only people who tend to volunteer for psychological experiments were so endowed? Or can we argue, as Kruglanski (1973), that only volunteers were sufficiently ego-involved in the tasks. Perhaps, but it seems more plausible to suppose that, in terms of subjects' ego-involvement, the experimental tasks were a distant second to the task of deciphering the meanings of their responses, and volunteers, who appear to be more inclined to please experimenters, gave the obvious, appropriate answers to suggest interest and ambition.

Volunteers, in general, seem to be more responsive to the experimenter's purposes. If the reader is thus led to question why so much data becomes confounded by role-related motives when the great majority of subjects are technically non-volunteers (Chapter 1), recall that several of the studies above showed that subjects with dispositions to volunteer, assessed on prior occasions, behaved similar to volunteers even when they were recruited for a course requirement.

DECEPTION

The practice of deceiving subjects about experimental purposes, though it seems to be linked to many of psychology's woes, is nevertheless inexorably tied to much of its method, particularly in the areas of social psychology and personality. Stricker (1967) found that 19 percent of studies reported in four leading journals of personality and social psychology in 1964 used *overt* deception (telling subjects deliberate untruths prior to the experiment). Menges (1973) reported that these figures for the year 1971 were 47 percent for *Journal of Personality and Social Psychology* and 22 percent for *Journal of Abnormal Psychology*. Neither survey included deception by *omission*, i.e., whereby subjects are deliberately given partial information in order to mislead them, which would probably boost these statistics considerably. From Menges' report we can ascertain that subjects were given complete and accurate information in less than 5 percent of studies in both journals, and that this figure was about the same in his study for *Journal of Experimental Psychology.*

Questions about the necessity of deception are reserved for the following chapter. Nor are we here concerned with ethical issues, for which the reader may consult: Baumrind (1964); Milgram (1964); Kelman (1967, 1972); Seeman (1969), Vinacke (1954); and Walster, Berscheid, Abrahem, and Aronson (1967). Our sole interest at this juncture is whether subjects once deceived become different in their role-related motives and behavior. On this question, Silverman (1965) has stated:

> I have had two experiences in trying to replicate data in May which I had obtained with Introductory Psychology students in September, which lead me to believe that I should choose one or the other month to do research. This did not come as a great surprise to me. If one is attuned to it, one can sense the temper of an introductory course subject population change from the beginning of the year to the end. The factor which I think is most instrumental is the 'briefing-debriefing' procedure which the student encounters sooner or later. Briefing means that he is told an untruth about what the experiment is about, and debriefing means that he is told that he was told an untruth, and then he is usually told a more innocuous untruth about what the experiment really was about. The effects of this on the subject-experimenter relationship can be likened to a marriage; one deception is all that is required, and forever after, if the husband says white, the wife will believe black.[1]

Silverman, Shulman, and Wiesenthal (1972) found support for these notions. They arranged that subjects who had participated for their first experiment in one involving deception and debriefing, or one that was completely straightforward, partook in the same second study about a week later. The latter study comprised four psychological tests, *all* of which discriminated significantly between groups. The tests and findings were:

---

[1] The author apologizes for the sex-role stereotypes inherent in the analogy. I would now, with benefit of the revelations of the past decade, substitute "deceiver" and "deceived" for "husband" and "wife."

1. The verb-noun test of compliance with demand characteristics (described in Chapter 3): Previously deceived subjects showed *less* compliance.
2. A standard-type persuasibility test, consisting of written arguments followed by opinion items: Deceived subjects were *more* persuaded.
3. The Rotter sentence completion test (Rotter & Rafferty, 1950), a projective measure of "maladjustment": Deceived subjects were *less* maladjusted.
4. The Gough and Heilbrun (1965) Adjective Check List: Differences between groups were significant at the 5 percent level on four of the 24 subscales, and at 10 percent for an additional six. For all of these ten scales, the self-ratings of the deceived subjects portrayed more favorable self-images.

The investigators had made some predictions about the pattern of results, based on the general concepts about subject roles discussed earlier. The experience of deception, they felt, would make subjects more alert to possible disguised meanings of their responses and the implications of these for their own self-presentation, and hence the deceived group was expected to show more favorable profiles on the two personality tests. The fact that these differences emerged on the projective as well as the self-report test suggest that these so-called projections are elicited on a more conscious level than is generally assumed.

It was considered that the verb-noun scale, which did not particularly provoke evaluation apprehension, could yield differences in either direction. Deceived subjects may have become more attuned to demand characteristics, but also may have become more non-compliant because of hostility or wariness about being "taken in." It appears that the latter occurred.

Similarly, no predictions were made for the persuasibility test, because attitude change in response to persuasive arguments can have a variety of connotations for subjects (Chapter 4). In the present case, it seems that the heightened sensitivity to evaluation of the deceived group was manifest in more agreement with the messages. Cook, Bean, Calder, Frey, Krovetz, and Reisman (1970) however, using a variation of the present design, found that deception in a prior experiment *decreased* persuasion. Whatever the reasons for this discrepancy, it illustrates again the vulnerability of attitude-change measures to whatever affects role-related motives.

THE EXPERIMENTER

Because of gross inattention by researchers to the feelings and intentions that are part of being a subject in a psychological experiment, they have ignored with equal passion the potential effects of the experimenter—the other party in this interaction—on these feelings and intentions. Our social psychological theories and our "conventional wisdom" tell us that people behave differently when interacting with different people, but the experimenter has traditionally been assumed to be as much a standardized factor in the experiment as the light fixtures in the laboratory. Silverman (1974) surveyed the authors of 262 applicable articles from three leading journals and found that in just 7 percent, experimenters were systematically varied across conditions and their effects were assessed. In 29 percent of these significant differences were found.

The experimenter has been less ignored in rhetoric than in practice. About every 15 years, it seems, someone has presented an impassioned argument for the existence of experimenter effects (Rosenzweig, 1933; Brunswick, 1947; McQuigan, 1963). In recent years there have been, in addition, numerous studies of the attributes of experimenters which differentially effect subject responses (some of which we have discussed in previous chapters), comprehensively reviewed by Rosenthal (1966) and Masling (1966). The studies compiled in these reviews showed influences of the experimenter's sex, age, race, religion, intelligence, birth order, anxiety, need for approval, hostility, authoritarianism, dominance, status, warmth, experience, prior acquaintanceship with the subject, relationship to the principal investigator, and attitude toward the research. The dependent variables in these studies have included measures of verbal learning, perceptual-motor performance, galvanic skin response, intelligence-test scores, susceptibility to influence, sensory deprivation effects, person perception, creative problem-solving, and a variety of attitudes, values, and personality traits assessed through projective tests, interviews, and questionnaires. A number of interactions have been found, both between experimenter attributes (e.g., sex and hostility, authoritarianism, and attitude toward the research) and between the same and different attributes in experimenters and subjects (e.g., race of experimenter and subject, anxiety level of experimenter, and sex of subject).

Later studies have also shown effects for attractiveness of female experimenters (Eisenman & Huber, 1970), sex-typing (masculinity-femininity) of both males and females (Shultz & Hartup, 1967), formality of the experimenter's dress and manner (Chapman, Chapman, & Brelje, 1969), and effects upon the dependent variable of pupillary dilation in response to sexual stimuli (Chapman, Chapman, & Brelje, 1969).

Experimenter characteristics may have homogeneous effects upon subjects; for example, higher status experimenters elicited projective test responses showing higher need for achievement (Birney, 1958) and "warmer" experimenters generated better performance on a test of signal detection (Ware, Kowal, & Baker, 1963). Or experimenter characteristics may differentially effect the dependent variable for different subject groups or conditions of the study; for example, Winkle and Sarason (1964) reported that verbal learning was increased for female, but not male, subjects when the experimenter was low test anxious; McQuigan (1963) compared four methods of learning, replicated across nine experimenters, and found a significant interaction on learning proficiency in which different methods were superior with different experimenters.

How does the personage or attributes of the experimenter modify his data? Probably by the variety of ways one person can covertly influence the behavior of another in an interaction, particularly if the interaction is almost completely dominated by the first party. The experimental manipulanda, after all, belong to the experimenter, and the subject's responses to them will probably reflect at least in part his responses to their owner. In the first example above, subjects probably "modeled" experimenters to some extent and, thus, showed higher need achievement scores in direct relation to their statuses. In the second, the experimenter who acted more warmly was probably better liked or made subjects feel more at ease; hence, they were more highly motivated to perform on his signal detection task. In the third, females may have been made more anxious by an anxious experimenter than males, with a consequent reduction in their verbal learning abilities; and in the last it is conceivable that each experimenter elicited the best performance with the learning method that he himself preferred, and was most enthusiastic or comfortable using.

Two processes by which experimenters influence their data, modeling and self-fulfilling prophecies, have been most widely studied, and these are discussed below.

MODELING

Several studies show that subjects tend to imitate their experimenters.

Klinger (1967) had actors play the roles of experimenters who were either achievement-oriented ("wore a suit and tie and the businesslike manner of an important achieving individual") or affiliation-oriented ("wore casual garb and manner, somewhat ingratiating and conciliatory ... sociably giving instructions"). Subjects of the achievement-oriented-actor-experimenters showed higher achievement-need scores on a T.A.T.-type test (McClelland et al., 1953) and the Gough and Heilbrun (1965) Adjective Check List. Subjects of affiliation-oriented-actor-experimenters had significantly higher scores on affiliation-related scales of the check list.

Marwit (1969) tape-recorded 20 research sessions, each comprised of a different experimenter and subject pair, and had both groups rated independently on seven personality dimensions. Correlations between ratings of experimenters and their subjects were significant on four dimensions, all in the positive direction.

Rosenthal (1966, pp. 119-122), using an indirect approach to modeling, examined the relationship between experimenters' performances and the mean performances of their subjects on his photo-rating projective measure of success-failure orientation. He reports ten such studies, spanning a five-year interval, with Ns of experimenters ranging from seven to 26. Six correlations were positive; however the remaining four were *negative* and of equivalent high order. The overall differences among correlations were significant at .006.

Other findings from Rosenthal (1966, pp. 62-86) were also orthogonal to the modeling hypothesis. Experimenters who were judged from films of their research sessions as "self-assured" and "dominant" obtained more failure-oriented responses from their subjects. Shulman and I, in 1965, found a significant *inverse* correlation between experimenters' test anxiety scores and those of their subjects, who were administered the inventory in groups of about 12, though we never did write about this finding.

Silverman, Shulman, and Wiesenthal (1972) had judges rate three male and three female experimenters on 22 personality trait scales from films of them interacting with subjects. (All experimenters in these filmed sessions saw the same subjects, who were actually confederates of the investigator.) At a later time, experimenters administered the same trait scales on which they had been rated to subjects, individually. Correlation coefficients were taken, separately for male and female experimenters interacting with male and female subjects, between two sets of difference scores, the difference between the mean judgments of any two experimenters on a given trait and the difference between the mean ratings made by the subjects of these experimenters on the same trait. Two of the four correlations were significant, those for same-sexed experimenter-subject dyads, but they were in opposite directions, positve for males and negative for females.

It appears that we are dealing with two distinct processes, modeling and something antithetical to modeling, but there are no hints from the data in general to suggest what conditions underlie each. Silverman et al. (1972) proposed that modeling may occur if aspects of the experimental situation, such as the status or power relationship between experimenter and subject or the likability of the experimenter, encourage identification by the subject. In the absence of identification, however, the subject may use the experimenter as a point of reference or comparison for his own self-evaluation or behavior, and this may yield the inverse relationships we have described. For example, in Rosenthal's various studies, to the extent that subjects were engaged in identification, consciously or otherwise, they would have shown more success-orientation with more confident and competent experimenters. To the extent that they did not identify, and they used the experimenter as a standard to assess their own levels of success-orientation, they would have shown less of the trait with more confident-seeming experimenters. In Silverman et al.'s study (1972), male subjects may have identified with males in the experimenter role, but not females interacting with females.

All of which speculation may be grist for some future researcher's mill, but is little aid to the experimenter who attempts to unravel the effects of himself from his independent variables.

SELF-FULFILLING PROPHECIES

To introduce the topic of meta-communication in the classroom, I have used a demonstration of "extrasensory perception" that works more often than it does not. I ask for a volunteer who has had experience communicating extrasensorily—there is usually at least one in a crowd—to come to the head of the room. He draws a playing card from the top of a deck with the picture cards removed, concentrates on the color as intensely as he can for a few seconds while the class focuses on his "thought transmissions," then asks them to write whether it is red or black. Then he concentrates on the number and asks them to write whether it is low (ace through five) or high (six through ten). He repeats this for about 10 to 20 cards, and then relates the correct choices. The class, overall, generally does better than chance; those who profess to believe in E.S.P. usually perform better than the rest; and those who do best on the first series or two tend, as a group, to continue at a high level. To practically insure success with the first "sender," I have him give feedback after each card for about 10 practice trials, but in order to keep the probability for each trial at 50 percent during the actual test, feedback must be given only at the end of a series.

I find that the most frustrating aspect of this exercise is convincing many afterward that the sender was covertly and unintentionally cueing the correct answers by para-language and gestures, and that those who were motivated by their own beliefs in the credibility of the venture were most apt to discriminate and respond to these cues.

Consider, then, the typical psychological experiment as an interaction between an experimenter who knows the responses the subject must give to support his hypothesis, and a subject who is attuned to any cues which will reduce ambiguity about what is expected of him. Robert Rosenthal did, and, in the *American Scientist* of 1963, described the first studies on the "experimenter-expectancy effect." These early studies used a number of photographs of people who were to be rated on the degree of success or failure they were experiencing, all of which had been prejudged to be neutral on this dimension. Student experimenters, however, were informed *either* that the photos had been found to elicit success or failure ratings, and they generally brought home the results they had been led to expect. The selection of this particular device, it should be noted, was not arbitrary. Rosenthal had originally used the task to measure projection as part of his doctoral dissertation (1956), and serendipitously became aware of his own biasing processes.

Within six years after Rosenthal's paper, there were nearly 100 reported studies on expectancy effects, extensively reviewed in Rosenthal (1969). Fifty-seven of these used the photo-rating task, and the remainder were distributed in the topical categories listed in

Table 5. (Photo-rating studies were listed as Person Perception.)

Possibly prompted by disbelievers, who maintained that conclusions about expectancy effects were often drawn from inadequate significance levels (Barber & Silver, 1968), Rosenthal (1969) performed an unprecedented analysis of the confidence levels that can be assumed from the data of all of the studies combined, for each topical area and overall. For this, he converted the probability value of each study to a z value from which he calculated a combined z value. In addition, he computed the proportions of studies with z values greater than or equal to 1.28 (which defines the 10 percent level).[2]

The results of these analyses are presented in Table 5. Confidence levels associated with z values for topical areas ranged from .03 for reaction time to one of one million squared for animal studies, and the cumulative z for all studies yielded a confidence level more infinitesimal than the latter. The percentage of studies which reached or exceeded z values of 1.28 greatly surpassed the 10 percent expected by chance in all areas. Even the consideration that the studies used may have been selective, in that those with negative results were less likely to be reported, does not much diminish our confidence in the effect. In a separate analysis, Rosenthal found that an unlikely 3,260 null replications would need to have been performed to reduce the overall z value to .05.

Paradoxically, then, what seems to be our sturdiest demonstration of a behavioral phenomenon pertains to artifact in the study of other phenomena.

What are the ways by which experimenter expectancies become translated into data? Again, there seem to be a host of possibilities. In studies using measures such as the photo-rating task, or an inkblot test, or psychophysical judgments, experimenters were generally led to expect a preponderance of one of two possible categories of response, such as success or failure ratings, few or many associations to inkblots (Marwit & Marcia, 1967), underestimations or overestimations of line lengths (Horst, 1966). The most obvious conjecture here is that experimenters covertly and selectively showed approval or disapproval to specific responses *during* the test (operant

---

[2] Modifications of this procedure were necessary for studies which did not simply compare the data of experimenters with opposed expectancies, for example, where a control group with no expectancies was used. These modifications were conservative in nature; that is, geared to a reduction of Type II errors, and are fully described in Rosenthal (1969).

Table 5. Expectancy effects in seven research areas

Research area	Studies	z	% ⩾ + 1.28
Animal learning	9	+8.64	100%
Learning and ability	9[a]	+3.01	44%
Psychophysical judgments	9[a]	+2.55	33%
Reaction time	3	+1.93	67%
Inkblot tests	4	+3.55	75%
Laboratory interviews	6[b]	+5.30	83%
Person perception	57[a, b]	+4.07	39%
All studies	94[c]	+9.82	50%

[a]Indicates a single experiment represented in each of three areas.

[b]Indicates a different experiment represented in each of two areas.

[c]Three entries were non-independent, and the mean z across areas was used for the independent entry.

Source: Adapted from Rosenthal, 1969, p. 299. Reprinted by permission.

conditioning by the trade name). Rosenthal (1966, pp. 289-293), however, found that expectancy effects were greater on his photo-rating measure for subjects' first responses than for later responses, and Adair and Epstein (1967) found expectancy effects on the same task when subjects spoke their ratings into a tape recorder without a live experimenter in the room. Apparently the experimenter can wield his influence, at least for this task, during the act of greeting and instructing the subject, though several attempts (Duncan & Rosenthal, 1968; Marwit, 1969) to clarify the processes by which this is accomplished fell short of success.

Expectancy effects in animal learning studies are easier to explain. Experimenters working with rats that they believed to be genetically superior handled them more frequently and gently, which would have enhanced performance, and also watched them more closely, which may have resulted in more rapid and accurate reinforcement (Rosenthal & Fode, 1963; Rosenthal & Lawson, 1964). Some of the human learning data might also be interpreted by an analogy of handling effects. Experimenters were led to expect better or poorer performance from subjects alleged to be more or less intelligent on abilities as diverse as problem-solving by mathematical reasoning (Hurvitz & Jenkins, 1966) and perceptual motor coordination measured by a marble-sorting test (Johnson, 1967). What probably happened in these studies was that supposedly more intelligent subjects were treated, in a variety of ways, as if they were more intelligent, and they responded accordingly.

Rosenthal and Jacobson (1968) found that similar effects occur in elementary school classrooms. Using fictitious scores on a test purported to reveal potential for "intellectual blooming," they instilled in California teachers expectancies for academic improvement for randomly selected children. At the end of the school year these children showed significantly higher mean increases in I.Q. than the rest. In ten further studies based on the Rosenthal and Jacobson procedure, five showed teacher expectancy effects (at the 10 percent confidence level), three others showed an interaction of teacher expectancy with some other variable—e.g., sex of pupil—and one showed an inverse effect (cf. Rosenthal, 1969, pp. 260-269).

Studies of reaction time illustrate another means by which experimenters' prophecies become self-fulfilled. Silverman (1968c) found that experimenters obtained longer association times for selected stimulus words from subjects whom they were led to expect would have more anxious conflict about these words. Experimenters might have accomplished this by a variety of uses of para-language, e.g., by looking at subjects suddenly before the critical words or systematically altering their vocal inflections. Silverman suggested that the same kind of biasing might be operative in studies using more sophisticated measures of conflict or anxiety, such as autonomic nervous system responses.

Expectancy effects have received more attention than any other single facet of artifact, perhaps because of the intrinsic interest of the phenomenon in the study of non-verbal communication and its implications for institutional relationships outside of the psychological experiment. In addition to Rosenthal and Jacobson's studies of teachers and pupils, Goldstein (1962) has amassed considerable evidence that expectancies given psychological practitioners regarding the potential for change of individual clients are important determinants of therapeutic success or failure.

6

Toward a Veridical Psychology

What do all of these revelations augur for the future of behavioral science? Perhaps very little.

S. Page (1975) conducted a survey recently of 250 research psychologists on their attitudes toward the literature about "the social psychology of the psychological experiment." Though 92 percent thought the discoveries needed to be taken seriously, just 26 percent could say they were "very familiar" with the area, 67 percent said that it had influenced their own research methods minimally or not at all, and 24 percent felt that psychology faced a methodological crisis.

It appears that confidence in the laboratory method has not much diminished, even among those who have taken the social psychology of the psychological experiment very seriously. "Tighter controls" is the panacea that is offered up regularly. Thus, Rosenberg has stated: "... the experimental method can readily be used to perfect, or at least to significantly improve itself. Any experimental demonstration of some source of systematic bias and of the process by which it operates immediately suggests procedures for the control and elimination of that source of bias" (1969, p. 347).

And from Orne: "In addition to the usual control procedures which are recognized as necessary in isolating the action of an independent variable in any experiment, studies with human subjects require a set of controls designed to look at the effect of the experimental technique itself" (1969, p. 177).

And Campbell's conclusion, in Rosenthal and Rosnow's (1969) collection of papers on artifact: "A major way in which this volume contributes to the science of psychological method is thus in establishing the need for new control groups" (1969, p. 358).

But how effective can these controls be? Let us examine the few visible influences of artifact research on current method. Psychologists seem to have become somewhat sensitive to experimenter-expectancy effects, perhaps because this is the simplest source of bias to deal with. More investigators, particularly in social psychology and personality, are using experimenters who are not aware of the hypotheses, or eliminating the experimenter as much as possible (e.g., by tape-recorded or written directions). But the experimenter's covert communications represent just one minor source of subjects' notions about the purposes of experiments; the procedures themselves provide far more viable cues and, further, to the extent that experiments are made impersonal we will need to confront the data of Jourard (1969) that anonymity of the experimenter discourages any sort of self-disclosure or naturalistic responding on the part of subjects.

The postexperiment "suspiciousness" interview or questionnaire has become more prominent as well. The assumptions here, however, are that subjects *can* correctly identify their hunches about the experiment's purposes and that they will reveal this information to the experimenter. Regarding the latter, the data discussed in Chapter 3 show very clearly that most will not. Thus, the practice of excluding the data of subjects who verbalize accurate suspicions, and assuming validity of the balance, will be frequently misleading. Further, as we have amply illustrated, correct identification of the experimental hypothesis is not a necessary or even important condition for confounding of data by role-related motives. Any feelings or notions about the experiment that systematically influence subjects' responses can lead to spurious conclusions.

QUASI-CONTROLS

The most extensive exposition of control procedures for role-related subject behavior comes from Orne (1969). Orne uses the term "quasi-controls" to refer to a simulation of the experiment without inclusion of the actual treatments, the data of which are compared to the data of the true experiment. The most apt illustration of quasi-controls is Orne and Scheibe's (1964) study of sensory deprivation (Chapter 3). Subjects who were led to believe they were experiencing sensory deprivation, but were not, showed similar effects to actually deprived subjects. For an example outside of Orne's laboratory, there is the study of color-sets by Hendrick, Wallace, and Tappenbeck (1968), also discussed in Chapter 3. When the object was surreptitiously removed from the visual field, subjects continued to report its presence, and showed the same effects of color-labeling on the amount of background coloration required before the object was reported as merged with the field as subjects in the actual experiment.

Both of these exercises in quasi-controls pointed to the influences of demand characteristics in prior studies. It taught us how *not* to do research on these questions, but not *how* to. Further, suppose that the results of the control studies were otherwise; subjects in pseudo-deprivation did not show deprivation effects and subjects reported that they no longer saw the object when it was removed. Would these data testify to the validity of the original experiments? Most certainly not. In the first case, they may simply mean that subjects can distinguish a fake from a real deprivation setting. Or it may be that subjects in real deprivation interpret their bodily experiences according to the way they think they should react, but some altered experience is necessary for there to be an interpretation. Similarly, the change in percept that occurs when an object is removed from a field is probably not the same as when it is gradually obscured by variations in background coloration, and if our hypothetical subjects reported its absence in the first instance, it does not mean that they were not influenced by demand characteristics in reporting its presence in the second instance. Quasi-controls can effectively demonstrate effects of role-related behavior; they cannot demonstrate the lack of such effects.

What we must recognize is that we are not dealing simply with "demand characteristics" or "evaluation apprehension" or "experimenter-expectancy effects," but a total, consuming set of feelings, attitudes, and intentions on the part of psychological subjects. These have been compartmentalized and labeled *extraneous factors*, which fit them neatly into our concepts of experimental control but, *from the subject's point of view, any small thing that he may do (if there is anything) that is not related to his role as such is indeed extraneous.*

Then the concept of control, as it is traditionally conceived, has no meaning for our problem. To control the influences of the subject's role-related behaviors, and thereby to eliminate their effects on his responses, is to eliminate his responses. As Orne has said, "Subjects are never neutral toward an experiment" (1969, p. 144), and the only way to neutralize them, or to assure that they are not behaving according to role, is to alter or remove the role.

ALTERING THE SUBJECT ROLE: THE SUBJECT AS ACTOR

As we suggested in Chapter 1, proposals for altering the subject role seem to hearken a return to introspectionism, when subject and experimenter were engaged in a collaborative effort, possessed of the same information about the nature and purpose of the study. Applied to contemporary psychological methods, introspectionism has taken the form of role-playing: subjects are exposed to the manipulanda of the experiment, but are told that they are manipulanda, and asked to try to respond as if they were real. Thus, Greenberg (1967) repeated Schacter's (1959) famous experiment on birth order and preference for affiliation in anxiety-provoking situations as a role-play, and found data comparable to the original. First-borns chose more than latter-borns to stay in the waiting room with others rather than alone, only in the condition when they anticipated painful shocks. Willis and Willis (1970), replicated the positive relationship between conformity and status of model with subjects who were made aware that the responses of the model were part of the experimenter's script.

Advocates of role-playing regard it as an alternative to deception, a strategy which elicits the active participation and cooperation of subjects and eliminates the motives which lead them to try to outthink the experimenter (Kelman, 1967; Ring, 1967; Schultz, 1969). But a closer look at our two illustrations reveals that this is not the case at all. Subjects in these studies were just *partial* collaborators of the experimenters, given just *some* of the information about the experiment. They were told nothing about the groups or conditions they would be compared to, nor about the meaning or purpose of their pretend activity. Hence, they were presented with as provocative a puzzle as subjects in the original studies. The major difference was that role-play subjects were spared deceptions by commission, and needed only to solve the deceptions by omission. Thus, the greater frequency of choices by first-borns to affiliate, when they were told the anxiety induction was contrived and when they were not, may represent in both cases their greater sensitivity to, or willingness to comply with, demand characteristics (in the previous chapter we described data showing that first-borns are, in fact, more likely to volunteer for experiments and that volunteers are more responsive to demand characteristics). Similarly, subjects may have shown more conformity to a make-believe high status model for the same reasons that they did for an alleged real one, because that is what they deduced the experimenter expected them to do.

Other writers (Aronson & Carlsmith, 1968; Freedman, 1969; Miller, 1972) have criticized the role-play strategy from a somewhat different viewpoint. They maintain, and correctly so, that for many areas of behavior, people are simply not able to guess what they would do until they do it. The more basic limitation, however, is that a participant in a role-play type experiment is *still in an experiment*, and the role of subject will take precedence over any other role that the experimenter wishes him to play.

REMOVING THE SUBJECT ROLE: NON-REACTIVE METHODS

We are drawn to conclude that virtually the only condition in which a subject in a psychological study will not behave as a subject is if he does not know he is one. This is psychology's "uncertainty principle"[1] and if we are to stop proliferating pseudo-data and move toward an authentic science, we must begin to regard it as seriously as do the physicists.

In one sense, we are better able to deal with our uncertainty principle than are the physicists, who might envy the fact that we can observe the substance of our science, behavior, in its natural state and create interventions in that state which duplicate naturalistic events. Microphysicists cannot make electrons react as if they were not in an experiment; psychologists *can* study behavior in subjects who are not aware that they are subjects. Methods which involve the total ignorance of the subject that he is part of an experiment may

---

[1] This analogy was recognized by the esteemed physicist Max Planck (1937, pp. 89-101).

be called "non-reactive" or "unobtrusive," after the terms used by Webb, Campbell, Schwartz, and Sechrest (1966), and will be discussed within several categories.

NATURALISTIC OBSERVATION

In the first paragraph of this book we noted that an important goal in the creation of psychology was to develop an experimental science of human behavior, in contrast to extant, descriptively oriented disciplines. In our naiveté, however, or enthusiasm for the task, we seem to have missed a critical point, that an experimental or laboratory science does not begin with the experiment or in the lab. If the reader will tolerate some unelaborate philosophy of science: Experiments are designed to test hypotheses, which are based on deductions from theoretical principles. But the development of viable theoretical principles requires a process of induction, and the material for induction generally comes from systematic observation of the phenomenon of interest as it naturally occurs. Similarly, the laboratory is used to study analogues of the phenomena in question, usually in the deductive, experimental phase, in order to manipulate and measure variables with rigorous control. The ultimate value of laboratory research, however, resides in the generalization of findings beyond the analogue, to the phenomenon in its naturalistic state.

Previously we stated that no one, to our knowledge, had ever put an animal conditioned in an operant paradigm in his natural habitat to see if he continued to make the responses that he learned, which is merely illustrative of a serious limitation in most psychological research. More often than not, the conclusions we draw from our laboratory studies pertain to the behavior of organisms in conditions of their own confinement and control and are probably generalizable only to similar situations (institutions, perhaps, such as schools or prisons or hospitals). The theories which spawn the research reflect the same focus on behavior under conditions of limited options.

Thus, I doubt whether the law of effect would have become the cornerstone of our theories of motivation and learning if we had begun our inquiries by watching children or monkeys or pigeons naturally develop and expand their potentials for interaction with their environments, an ongoing and consuming process which occurs in people and animals who are not deprived of food or water or attention and who are not necessarily rewarded by external agents for specific responses. Nor can we explain why it took so many decades before motivation researchers grudgingly accepted the concept of curiosity into their lexicon, unless they studiously excluded their day-to-day observations of children and other young animals from their theory-making. Social psychologists have conducted countless studies on the topic of small-group processes, but very few dealt with the nature and function of people's groupings in their day-to-day lives. Rather, the theories and data came almost exclusively from studies of artificial groups performing artificial tasks in artificial settings, all imposed on subjects by experimenters.

Behavioral scientists seem peculiarly inattentive to the behavior which surrounds them. It is almost as if we have formed an implicit rule that the scientific study of behavior requires that we isolate it from its natural contexts, and so we construct theories that provide deductions that are testable in tightly controlled, but unnatural contexts.

My favorite query on dissertation oral examinations is how the investigator came to believe that the aspects of behavior he chose to examine or the concepts that guided his research were important. Was he led, for example, to study modeling in children because he discovered that children do a great deal of modeling? Or did his interest in attitude formation come from long-standing fascination with public opinion trends, or from some provocative phenomenon he observed listening to people of different opinions trying to persuade each other? The question usually evokes a blank stare, and it turns out that their concepts came from someone else's concepts, which probably came from someone else's concepts, and at no stage in the process did anyone take a serious look at life. Of course, there are the invariable attempts at the close of journal articles to extrapolate findings to natural occurring behavior—feeble attempts, evidenced by the lack of impact of some 100 years of psychology on the human condition, *because the efforts never began in life.*

Willems (1969) in his excellent presentation of a rationale for naturalistic research describes a number of cases in point. For example, much experimentation with children has focused on the deleterious effects of frustration, and the concepts that emerged have become central to our theories of personality development. Fawl (1963), however, analyzed records of continuous, naturalistic observations of children compiled at the Midwest Psychological Field Station of the University of Kansas and found that frustration, defined in terms of blocked goals, did not customarily produce any observable reaction, and when disturbances did occur, they were mild in intensity. Hovland (1959), in his discussion of discrepancies between laboratory and field data on persuasion, concluded that attitudes in life remained more stable than experimental evidence would suggest because people selectively exposed themselves to communications which were congruent to their positions.

Ethologists, on the other hand, were devoted to naturalistic observation long before psychology existed as a discipline. Though traditionally they have focused almost exclusively on subhuman species, there is a burgeoning interest both on the part of ethologists (e.g., Eibl-Eibesfeldt, 1970; Tinbergen, 1974) and psychologists (e.g., Bowlby, 1969; Sommer, 1969) in applying their methods and concepts of research to human behavior. This is a trend that may represent a turning point for psychology. When we have compiled a proportionally equivalent volume of descriptive data about the naturalistic, ongoing activities of people as ethologists have about ring doves or Himalayan baboons, we may then be led to viable theories and methods for discovering the important contingencies of human behavior.

ARCHIVAL RESEARCH

Though the major activity of psychologists is the recording of behavior, we seem to have virtually ignored the fact that man, since antiquity, has continuously kept copious records of every sort about himself. Psychologists have largely bypassed archival data, perhaps because of their obsession with rigor. Records are subject to many sources of bias and error and an archival study cannot be precisely replicated. But laboratory research is also subject to many sources of bias and error, and replication may establish the reliability of a spurious finding as well as a valid one. For example, we showed in Chapter 4 that many similar experiments have claimed to support a causal relationship between frustration and minority group prejudice, but any or all of these findings may have been based on reactions of subjects to experimenters rather than minority group members, as demonstrated in Silverman and Kleinman (1967). On the other hand, perhaps the most widely cited and durable finding regarding frustration and prejudice was Hovland and Sears' (1940) much earlier report of a highly significant inverse correlation between recorded indices of economic stability and the number of lynchings of blacks by whites in the southeastern United States. Of course, archival research is necessarily descriptive and subject to alternative causal explanations (e.g., the transgressions which led to lynchings may have been higher during periods of economic instability), but we may have generated more insight about frustration and prejudice by pursuing records further to establish the credence of alternative explanations, rather than embarking on a series of questionable experiments.

For most of the archival research that has been reported (cf. Webb, Campbell, Schwartz, & Sechrest, 1966), the variables of interest were contained in the records themselves, for example, studies of the effects of various types of political campaigns on voting behavior, or shelf positions of supermarket items on sales, or employment conditions on job turnover, etc. A number of other studies, however, illustrate the potential use of records as powerful, non-reactive measures for the exploration of deeper theoretical questions.

For example, Bain and Hecock (1957) found evidence for a "primacy effect" for alternative choices in a study of the order of candidates' names on a ballot and the votes they received. They were able, in fact, to construct a field experiment (defined later) by using statistics from a state which required systematic rotations of names on the ballot. DeCharms and Moeller (1962) demonstrated a relationship which should have been of considerable interest to theories of motivation and modeling, between achievement imagery in children's readers and numbers of patents issued over a 150-year period. Coleman, Katz, and Menzel (1957) consulted pharmacy records to establish that adoptions of new drugs by physicians followed patterns predictable from their social networks according to concepts of reference group identification. Principles of reward, punishment, and extinction were tested by Ashley (1962) from stockmarket statistics. He found that the positive effect on prices of an unexpectedly high dividend or earnings statement persisted about four times longer than the negative effect of an unexpectedly low dividend or statement. Dornbusch and Hickman (1959) used content analyses of magazine advertisements to test hypotheses about generational changes in "other-directedness." Osgood and Walker (1959) compared suicide notes with control notes to examine deductions from the Hull-Spence theory of dominant response activation, predicting that the motivation of suicidal persons should increase the dominant responses in their hierarchy and, in turn, the stereotypic nature of their communications. Sechrest and Olson (1966) used graffiti on toilet walls to study conditions related to minority group prejudice. Doob, Carlsmith, Freedman, Landauer, and Tom (1969) tested some major deductions from dissonance theory by comparing sales of a product in different stores in relation to how much the product had been previously discounted in price. From the same theory, Verbruggen (1973) was able to make successful "post-dictions" about the positions and arguments of various chemists in the 18th century regarding the phlogiston controversy.

THE FIELD "EXPERIMENT"

The term field experiment has acquired a variety of meanings, though, by the classic definition, it is not an experiment at all. It is a descriptive study whereby the investigator utilizes a naturalistic occurrence which resembles the treatment he would have created in his laboratory to test a hypothesis of cause-effect relationship. Perhaps the most widely known field experiment by this definition is Festinger, Rieken, and Schacter's (1956) "When prophecy fails." Here the investigators tested predictions about the effects of expectancy-disconfirmation by observing the activities of a group of religious zealots who made extensive preparations for the demise of the world before and after the date on which the event was anticipated. Another illustration comes from Goldman, Jaffa, and Schacter's (1968) tests of hypotheses about differential stimuli for the eating behavior of normal and obese persons, by comparing the experiences of religious Jews in these categories on the Day of Atonement (Yom Kippur), for which a 24-hour fast is obligatory. Zucker, Manosevitz, and Lanyon (1968) examined the proposition that first-borns tend more to affiliate when stressed than latter-borns by interviews and observations during a two-day power failure in New York City. Knox and Inkster (1968) investigated the effects of commitment to a decision by polling horse-bettors about their confidence in their choices several seconds before or after they reached the betting window, and Mann and Taylor (1969) studied the effects of motives on perception by asking people to estimate the numbers of people who were waiting ahead of them on various queues.

Though we could continue to list examples, the field experiment is not, by any means, a commonly used strategy, despite the fact that it offers the researcher the opportunity to approximate experimental conditions without the qualifications that adhere to behavioral data acquired in a laboratory. One reason may be that these are not truly experiments, the independent variables cannot be isolated from other causal factors with the same precision that is obtained if the experimenter maintains control of his treatments. But one would assume that, given the confidence in generalization that is gained by working in natural settings, field experiments would be used more often than they are, at least in conjunction with laboratory research. A more salient reason, perhaps, is that field experiments require a longer time of search and wait than laboratory studies. It is often simpler and potentially less frustrating to construct a laboratory analogue of an event than to search and/or wait for it to appear under natural conditions in a form whereby it can be studied.

THE EXPERIMENT IN THE FIELD

This represents, in a sense, the most elegant of unobtrusive research strategies inasmuch as it is the only one that is experimental. Manipulations and measurements are carried out in naturalistic settings, however, and as a rule, subjects are not aware at any time that they are part of a study. It appears, on the basis of one survey of recent journal articles (Cook, 1973) and several current texts and collections (Bickman & Henchy, 1972; Evans & Rozelle, 1970; Snadowsky, 1972; Webb, Campbell, Schwartz, & Sechrest, 1962; Willems & Rausch, 1969), that experiments in the field are becoming increasingly popular, particularly in the areas of personality and social psychology.

The topic which has been most extensively studied by these techniques is help-giving behavior, perhaps because it is well suited or because interest in the topic coincided with increasing interest in naturalistic experimentation. Some of these experiments were rather simplistic and atheoretical in nature. For example, Latané (1970) had students ask assistance of various kinds from passersby, varying the sex and aspects of the approach of the solicitee. Gaertner and Bickman's (1972) experimenters phoned subjects, pretending to have reached a wrong number using their last piece of change in a public phone on a highway, trying to get help because their car was disabled. The party was asked to phone the caller's garage and ask them to come for him, but the garage number was actually the experimenter's phone, and a confederate was standing by to take the message. The variable of interest was race; subjects in distinctly black and white neighborhoods in New York City were called by black or white experimenters with distinctive voice characteristics. Race was also the independent variable of a study by Wispé and Freshley (1971) who arranged for a black or white female experimenter's bag of groceries to tear open in front of a supermarket, spilling the contents.

Other experiments, however, have had a theoretical base. Bryan and Test (1967) did a series of studies on modeling effects by, for example, creating conditions whereby people approaching a Salvation Army kettle were either exposed or not exposed to an experimental confederate making a donation. Hornstien, Masor, Sole, and Heilman (1971) tested derivations from theory about the "Zeigarnik Effect." To see whether people were more likely to complete the interrupted goal-directed activity of others when the goal was closer to attainment, they placed open stamped addressed envelopes where they would appear to have been mislaid, containing a contribution for medical research and a form indicating this was either the sender's second or ninth contribution in a ten-payment plan.

Experiments in the field have been used in a variety of other areas as well. To illustrate: Leventhal and Niles (1964) tested Janis and Feshbach's (1953) hypotheses regarding fear and persuasion (described in Chapter 5) by showing films about lung cancer, varying in fear-arousal value, to different audiences at a health exposition and noting the numbers of people in each group who stopped for chest X rays. Morse and Gergen (1970) studied the effects of social comparison on self-esteem by soliciting job applicants and arranging for them to casually encounter a person whose characteristics were either socially desirable or undesirable prior to filling out an application form dealing with their self-concepts. Byrne, Ervin, and Lamberth (1970) organized a computer dating service in a university to investigate some tenets of attraction research. They matched couples for a brief liaison on the basis of various dimensions ascertained from their applications, and then took measures of attraction, including the physical proximity of the partners during a post-date interview. Doob and Gross (1968), in a study of status as a mediator of aggression, had different quality automobiles delay at red lights and recorded the amount of time before the driver behind sounded his horn, and the duration and frequency of horn-honking. Deci (1971) investigated the effects of external rewards on intrinsic motivation by arranging a stipend for one group of "headline-writers" for a college newspaper and comparing the time given the task to their previous unpaid performances and to an unpaid control group.

CONDITIONS FOR VALID REACTIVE RESEARCH

We have tried to be emphatic in developing a rationale for non-reactive research, but we do not mean to imply that a total commitment of psychology to these strategies is either feasible or advisable. Undoubtedly there are many questions which can be answered with research designs in which subjects are briefed with total frankness and the responses required of them are sufficiently simplistic and unambiguous so that role-related motives are irrelevant. One can, for example, confidently assess the data of a carefully controlled experiment on the effects of drugs on reaction times, or the punctate distribution of skin sensitivity to warmth or cold. Thus, non-reactive methods may have limited value for areas in which constructs and their operations are relatively narrow in scope and definition, such as perception and psychophysiology, though we have illustrated potential pitfalls based on subject roles in some of these studies as well.

Then, too, there are methods directed to more molar questions, using knowing subjects, which may nevertheless yield authentic data. Valid contributions have come from well-planned interviews and case studies such as Kinsey, Pomeroy, and Martin's (1948) pioneering investigations of sexual behavior, or, more recently, Fellner and Marshall's (1970) studies of the decision processes of kidney donors. The research questions posed by these investigators allowed them to approach the subject in a straightforward and honest manner to solicit information directly about an area of behavior of much relevance to himself. Though, even under these conditions, respondents were probably somewhat affected by concerns about their images and the interviewers' expectations, one can assume that their primary motives were for sincere cooperation and communication. Honest cooperation by subjects may be achieved, as well, in extended studies in which the investigator functions as a participant-observer in a naturalistic setting, such as the observations conducted over years by Sherif and Sherif (1964) of reference group identification and behavior in adolescent groups.

THE SOCIALIZATION OF PSYCHOLOGISTS

These suggestions are not intended to represent a panacea for psychology's problems. They comprise an attempt to answer the reader who has accepted the thesis of this book and asks: "Where do we go from here?" They offer approaches to behavioral research which obviate the most profound sources of artifact in the present methods, modest proposals of means to begin a science of behavior from data that is veridical and generalizable. We can probably not generate much intelligent insight about where that beginning will take us until we do, in fact, seriously begin.

But beyond questions about specific methodologies is the wider issue of the socialization of psychologists. Given their unquestioned superior analytical abilities, psychologists as a group must be subject to some peculiar processes of indoctrination and self-delusion to perpetuate models for research with such transparent flaws. Some conjectures about these processes are offered below.

CURIOSITY

Students generally come to their first psychology course with a good deal of curiosity about human behavior, and begin to learn almost immediately that this is not the place where that motive will be nurtured or even indulged. Consider the following hypothetical but prototypic interaction between undergraduate and professor.

Student: "For my research project . . . I'd like to study how people pick the people that they marry. I want to interview couples who are married or about to be married and ask them why they picked that partner over anyone else. . . . What was the most important thing for them about the other person? . . . Whether it was an easy decision or not? . . . Whether one person had to persuade the other or were they both just as eager? . . . Questions like that . . ."

Professor: "Well, that's an interesting topic, but you need to do a bit of *groundwork* before you begin actual research. There is a *scientific method,* and there are certain procedures that you must follow. First, you must do a *literature search,* to know the existing work in the *area* related to your topic. Now, the area you seem to be interested in is *interpersonal attraction.* I'll give you the titles of some books to start you off, then you can consult the *Psychological Abstracts* for a more complete *bibliography.* Now, from your literature search you should emerge with *theory* pertaining to your topic, from which you may deduce *hypotheses*, such as '*Attraction of a person to another as a marital partner is positively related to similarity of attitudes.*' Or, if you want to do *exploratory research*, you still require a *conceptual framework* from which to pose a question. An example of such a question is '*What is the relationship between selection of marital partners and propinquity?*' Then you need to *operationally define* your *variables*, perhaps do some *validation studies* of your operational definitions, *design* your research with appropriate *control conditions*, decide about your *sampling techniques, statistical analyses, confidence levels*, etc., etc., etc., etc. ...."

Be assured that the writer does not lack due respect for literature searching, theory, hypotheses, control procedures, statistics, etc., but note how effectively the student was diverted *away* from the behavior which piqued his curiosity into rituals of abstraction and procedure from which he will probably never return.

Consider, not entirely for fun, the probable response of a typical Ph.D. dissertation committee if they had received a proposal from Jean Piaget that read: "The investigator's intention is to watch his children methodically over an extended period of time, taking copious notes on their activities, to see if he can learn something about how they learn."

This process of socialization was made vivid to me recently at the M.A. oral examination of a student whom I had known well in his undergraduate years, who had worked in various non-professional capacities with children, and who, I recalled, was intensely interested in their behavior and development. His thesis was an elaboration of previous work by his thesis supervisor on "reliability and validity of interpersonal perceptions of dominance hierarchies in preschoolers." I asked him at the examination what he was *really* interested in, what it was that he was curious about in children or dominance that had led him to this specific study. He answered, seemingly pleased to be able to talk about it, that he had always been fascinated by how children developed their different styles of interaction, particularly with regard to power relationships. Then I asked how his study had brought him closer to an understanding of these behaviors, and he proceeded to relate anecdotes about interactions among the children in his sample which were not described in any of his tables or graphs and had no direct bearing on his thesis. I pointed this out and suggested that he might have gotten closer to the questions that generated his interest by simply hanging around groups of children for a while, recording and pondering his observations, but, of course, that M.A. proposal may have encountered some difficulty. I await with morbid curiosity his Ph.D. thesis which may be titled "Effects of experimental interventions in the interpersonal perceptions of dominance hierarchies in preschoolers." And another career is underway.

To begin to build an authentic psychology, we need people in our midst who are made restless and agitated by the puzzlements in the human condition. We must guide them into sophisticated and productive channels for their curiosities, but never suppress them. Without nurturance of curiosity, the training we administer in rigor and exactitude will contribute nothing to the development of our science but a further proliferation of pseudo-research.

PRIORITIES

Unlike other disciplines, most general psychology texts begin with an elaborate justification of the right of psychology to be called a science, usually by describing the nature of scientific method, with at least a few examples from physics or biology, and by demonstrating that the activities of psychologists are basically the same. If psychology has a problem in its relationship to science in general, however, it is not that it is too much *unlike* other disciplines but that it is too much *like* them. Within the wide spectrum of epistemological strategies that constitute acceptable "science," uniformities can be reduced to three: the assumption of determinism, the aim of establishing relationships among events, and the method of empiricism. Given these "requirements" of science every discipline has its own priorities, which may depend on the nature of its substance and/or the stage of its inquiry. Astronomy demands precise description; it exists without benefit of the experiment. Electron physicists found it beneficial to abandon theory in favor of mathematically based prediction. Psychologists need not consider it a compromise with science to recognize that their *highest priority*, particularly at this exploratory stage of inquiry, is the *generalization value* of their findings to naturally-occurring behavior. Yet it is the aspect we have chosen to emphasize the least. Hence we have the spectacle of a science of behavior in which investigators count flashing lights and ponder computer print-outs and very rarely find themselves watching people do what they naturally do—in which the major concerns of researchers are the availability of subjects, and laboratory space to bring them to, and rarely are about where the behavior that they want to study is happening and how they can study it while keeping it reasonably intact.

TIME PERSPECTIVES

Ask people foreign to our field what they would logically surmise to be the modal time for data collection for published psychological studies. Answers would probably be in months, or years, but perusals of journals show that it is probably several hours at most.

All of our pedagogical activities seem oriented to the propagation of short-term, expediently administered, laboratory analogue-type studies. Naturally, precision of measurement and control becomes the principal priority—one must be precise if he is going to generate knowledge about personality development or learning processes in a few hours—and generalization value occupies the lowest priority.

The student entering his M.A. program expects that he must, in addition to course work, assistantships, etc., become thoroughly acquainted with an area of research, propose and have approved a conceptually based study, collect, analyze and interpret data, and present a written thesis, preferably within a year. Certainly if he takes longer than two he will be looked at askance. I had a typical interaction recently with an M.A. student who showed me a paper she had prepared on predisposing and precipitating factors in suicide, which I thought was quite good. She wanted to work on these ideas toward her M.A. and I told her that the only feasible way to approach her questions would be to try, through appropriate agencies, to reach people who had attempted suicide or had been close to people who committed suicide, probe into each history to establish the extent to which the predisposing and precipitating factors were present, and compare these to a group of matched controls. She did not think I was serious. I expect that she will return to me, or someone else, with appropriately disguised paper and pencil inventories of the predisposing and precipitating variables, and a similar scale to measure tendencies toward suicide, all capable of being administered to 200 plus undergraduates within an hour. Then if someone writes a sequel to this book, they can comment that her correlations were probably based on some latent factor, like mood of the subject at the time of testing. And it is not that she is a poor student; in fact, she is one of the best. For a student to undertake a study of that magnitude at her level would be so counter to norms and expectations that even the best usually find projects that generate maximum data yields for minimum expenditures of time and effort.

The Ph.D. dissertation is generally more of the same, with each step somewhat exaggerated. True, the student has more time, but the same set of norms and expectations are operating, and he has already been pretty much socialized to them. Moreover, his Master's work has not given him any basis in data or other impetus to pursue a long-term project. So his doctoral thesis becomes the second in a series of micro-endeavors. Then there are publications toward tenure and promotions to consider and by the time the implicit and explicit pressures on him *not* to do something with generalization value have subsided, he is usually too far into the system to emerge.

SIGNIFICANT DIFFERENCES AND INSIGNIFICANT RESEARCH

A prime feature of the student's socialization for exactitude is his introduction into the realm of inferential statistics. It is taken as dogma by most students (probably because it has been taught as such) that scientific studies demand statistical tests of differences, and that differences which do not achieve the .05 (or preferably the .01) levels of significance cannot be admitted as evidence for a phenomenon. The inquisitive student may ask why differences with a probability value of chance occurrence of 15 or even 20 percent are not worth communicating, especially if they pertain to important questions, and he will usually be told that the traditional conservatism of scientific method deems it so. It is undoubtedly noticed, but probably few students possess the self-assurance to take it seriously, that the profound contributors to psychological knowledge—Freud, Darwin, Pavlov, Wertheimer, Piaget, Kohler, Lorenz, Lashley, etc.—worked largely without benefit of statistical tests. The student may gain some assurance from the following paragraphs by Lipset,

Trow, and Coleman explaining why statistical tests were not employed in their study.

> This study, like many in social science, is an exploratory study, not a confirmatory one, while statistical tests of hypotheses are designed for confirmation ... to confirm and consolidate what is already believed to be true. A study like the present one is designed to find out what was not even guessed at before. That this new knowledge is not fully confirmed is no great cause for concern. Further studies upon different organizations will constitute more reliable confirmation, for they test the hypotheses in a different population, which a Chi-square test used on this data could never do. It is probably better to place one's faith in further studies to confirm hypothesized relationships than to place it in Chi-square tests. ... This is the method through which the natural sciences have made most of their remarkable advances, and there is no indication that these advances would have come earlier if modern statistical inference had been used instead. ...
>
> For example, a careful reading of W.P.D. Wightman's *The Growth of Scientific Ideas* (1953), which charts the course of scientific discoveries from early times, failed to show more than one or two possible places where statistical inference might have contributed significantly to the development of any science in its early years. (1956, pp. 430-431)*

Statistical tests, and particularly stringent confidence levels, have their principal utility when investigations in an area are deep in the deductive phase, where experiments are sequential with the findings of each, crucial to decisions about the next. A veridical psychology, however, must take its roots in inductive research, where the emphasis is on discovery rather than confirmation. This does not imply that statistical tests cannot be usefully applied in *some* exploratory studies (where they are probably best used without strict requirements for confidence levels), but our regard of such tests as *sine qua non* for scientific method has directed us away from discovery-oriented research into confirmation-oriented research.

Psychology's slavish adherence to statistical tests is another re-

*Reprinted by permission.

flection of its misguided attempt to gain the appearance of scientific respectability. We display our statistical acumen with great relish. Our rites of passage through all of the levels to the Ph.D. contain progressively difficult requirements regarding statistics, which are the most general and frequently the only requirements, without options, that we have. Students become impressed, which I suspect is a large part of our purpose, with the mastery of meta-language and technique that is needed to be a scientific psychologist, but they also come to believe from all of our methods of indoctrination that sophistication of statistical analyses is an indicator of sophistication of research. And this detracts from our effort rather than enhances it, for significant differences based on insignificant studies will continue to take us nowhere.

IN SUM

We are not prevented by external restraints from building a veridical, scientific psychology. The means to begin are, and always have been, within our grasp. They will remain in abeyance, however, as long as the culture of psychology is unchanged. I beg the question of how our culture will change; it is not subject to prescription. There is no formula to offer for constructing a psychology in which curiosity is directed into productive channels, generalization-value is given at least as high a priority as precision, time perspectives are appropriate to the nature of the questions that we seek to answer, and attempts at discovery are treated as respectfully as attempts at confirmation. These changes depend on attitudes and if this book has altered attitudes in any small way, if it has made us somewhat less comfortable with our traditions, then it has been worth the effort.

References

Abelson, R.P., Aronson, E., McGuire, W.J., Newcomb, T.M., Rosenberg, M.J., & Tannenbaum, P.H. (Eds.)ᴇ *Theories of cognitive consistency: A sourcebook.* New York: Rand McNally, 1968.

Adair, J.G., & Epstein, J. Verbal cues in the mediation of experimenter bias. Paper presented at the meeting of the Midwestern Psychological Association, Chicago, May 1967.

Anderson, O.D. An experimental study of observational attitudes. *American Journal of Psychology,* 1930, **42,** 345-369.

Archer, E.J., Cejka, J., & Thompson, C.P. Serial-trigram learning as a function of differential meaningfulness and sex of subjects and experimenters. *Canadian Journal of Psychology,* 1961, **15,** 148-153.

Argyris, C. Some unintended consequences of rigorous research. *Psychological Bulletin,* 1968, **70,** 185-197.

Aronson, E., & Carlsmith, J.M. Experimentation in social psychology. In G. Lindzey & E. Aronson (Eds.), *Handbook of social psychology.* Vol. 2. Reading, Mass.: Addison-Wesley, 1968.

Aronson, E., Carlsmith, J.M., & Darley, J.M. The effects of expectancy on volunteering for an unpleasant experience. *Journal of Abnormal and Social Psychology,* 1963, **66,** 220-224.

Asch, S.E. Studies of independence and conformity: I. A minority of one against a unanimous majority. *Psychological Monographs: General and Applied,* 1956, **70,** No. 9 (Whole No. 416).

Ashley, J.W. Stock prices and changes in earnings and dividends: Some empirical results. *Journal of Political Economy*, 1962, **70**, 82-85.

Ashley, W.R., Harper, R.S., & Runyan, D.K. The perceived size of coins in normal and hypnotically induced economic states. *American Journal of Psychology*, 1951, **64**, 564-592.

Babladelis, G. Personality and verbal conditioning effects. *Journal of Abnormal and Social Psychology*, 1961, **62**, 41-43.

Bain, H.M., & Hecock, D.S. *Ballot position and voter's choice: The arrangement of names on the ballot and its effect on the voter.* Detroit: Wayne State University Press, 1957.

Barber, T.X. Measuring "hypnotic-like" suggestibility with and without "hypnotic induction"; Psychometric properties, norms, and variables influencing response to the Barber Suggestibility Scale (BSS). *Psychological Reports*, 1965, **16**, 809-844.

Barber, T.X. *Suggested ("hypnotic") behavior: The trance paradigm versus an alternative paradigm.* Harding, Mass.: Medfield Foundation, 1970.

Barber, T.X., & Calverley, D.S. The definition of the situation as a variable affecting "hypnotic-like" suggestibility. *Journal of Clinical Psychology*, 1964, **20**, 438-440. (a)

Barber, T.X., & Calverley, D.S. Empirical evidence for a theory of "hypnotic" behavior: Effects of pretest instructions on response to primary suggestions. *Psychological Record*, 1964, **14**, 457-467. (b)

Barber, T.X., & Silver, M.J. Fact, fiction, and the experimenter bias effect. *Psychological Bulletin Monograph Supplement*, 1968, **70**, 1-29.

Baumrind, D. Some thoughts on ethics of research: After reading Milgram's "Behavioral Study of Obedience." *American Psychologist*, 1964, **19**, 421-423.

Berkowitz, L. The frustration-aggression hypothesis revisited. In L. Berkowitz (Ed.), *Roots of aggression: A re-examination of the frustration-aggression hypothesis.* New York: Atherton Press, 1968.

Berkowitz, L., & LePage, A. Weapons as aggression-eliciting stimuli. *Journal of Personality and Social Psychology*, 1967, 7, 202-207.

Bickman, L., & Henchy, T. (Eds.) *Beyond the laboratory: Field research in social psychology.* New York: McGraw-Hill, 1972.

Birney, R.C. The achievement motive and task performance: A replication. *Journal of Abnormal and Social Psychology*, 1958, **56**, 133-135.

Bowlby, J. *Attachment and loss. Vol. I. Attachment.* London: Hogarth, 1969.

Brehm, J.W. *A theory of psychological reactance.* New York: Academic Press, 1966.

Brunswick, E. Systematic and representative design of psychological experiments with results in physical and social perception. (Syllabus Series No. 304) Berkeley: University of California Press, 1947.

Bryan, J.H., & Lichtenstein, E. Effects of subject and experimenter attitude in verbal conditioning. *Journal of Personality and Social Psychology,* 1966, **3,** 182-189.

Bryan, J.H., & Test, M.A. Models and helping: Naturalistic studies in aiding behavior. *Journal of Personality and Social Psychology,* 1967, **6,** 400-407.

Budner, S. Individual predisposition and external pressure: A note on determination of attitudes. *Journal of Social Psychology,* 1960, **51,** 145-156.

Byrne, D. The Repression-Sensitization Scale: Rationale, reliability, and validity. *Journal of Personality,* 1961, **29,** 334-349.

Byrne, D. Repression-sensitization as a dimension of personality. In B.A. Maher (Ed.), *Progress in experimental personality research.* New York: Academic Press, 1964, pp. 169-220.

Byrne, D., Ervin, C.R., & Lambreth, J. Continuity between the experimental study of attraction and real-life computer dating. *Journal of Personality and Social Psychology,* 1970, **16,** 157-165.

Campbell, D.T. Prospective: Artifact and control. In R. Rosenthal & R.L. Rosnow (Eds.), *Artifact in behavioral research.* New York: Academic Press, 1969, pp. 351-382.

Carey, G.L. Sex differences in problem-solving performance as a function of attitude differences. *Journal of Abnormal and Social Psychology,* 1958, **56,** 256-260.

Cataldo, J.F., Silverman, I., & Brown, J.M. Demand characteristics associated with semantic differential ratings of verbs and nouns. *Educational & Psychological Measurement,* 1967, **27,** 83-87.

Chapman, L.J., Chapman, J.P., & Brelje, T. Influence of the experimenter on pupillary dilation to sexually provocative pictures. *Journal of Abnormal Psychology,* 1969, **74,** 396-400.

Cochran, W.G., Mosteller, F., & Tukey, J.W. Statistical problems of the Kinsey report. *Journal of the American Statistical Association,* 1953, **48,** 673-716.

Cohen, B.H. Role of awareness in meaning established by classical conditioning. *Journal of Experimental Psychology*, 1964, **67**, 373-378.

Coleman, J., Katz, E., & Menzel, H. The diffusion of an innovation among physicians. *Sociometry*, 1957, **20**, 253-270.

Cook, T.D. Thoughts on the potential and limitations of field experiments. Presented at the symposium titled "Getting clean data from dirty situations: Control and significance of bias in experiments." American Psychological Association, Montreal, Quebec, 1973.

Cook, T.D., Bean, J., Calder, B., Frey, R., Krovetz, M., & Reisman, S. Demand characteristics and three conceptions of the frequently deceived subject. *Journal of Personality and Social Psychology*, 1970, 14, 185-194.

Cowen, E., Landes, J., & Shaet, D.E. The effects of mild frustration on the expression of prejudiced attitudes. *Journal of Abnormal and Social Psychology*, 1959, **58**, 33-39.

Criswell, J. The psychologist as perceiver. In R. Tagiuri & L. Petrullo (Eds.), *Person perception and interpersonal behavior.* Stanford: Stanford University Press, 1958, 95-119.

Crowne, D.P., & Marlowe, D. *The approval motive.* New York: Wiley, 1964.

Crowne, D.P., & Marlowe, D. A new scale of social desirability independent of psychopathology. *Journal of Consulting Psychology*, 1960, **24**, 349-354.

Crowne, D.P., & Strickland, B.R. The conditioning of verbal behavior as a function of the need for social approval. *Journal of Abnormal and Social Psychology*, 1961, **63**, 395-401.

Crutchfield, R.S. Conformity and character. *American Psychologist*, 1955, **10**, 191-198.

Dabbs, J.M., & Janis, I. Why does eating while reading facilitate opinion change?—An experimental inquiry. *Journal of Experimental Social Psychology*, 1965, **2**, 133.

Damaser, E.C., Shor, R.E., & Orne, M.T. Physiological effects during hypnotically requested emotions. *Psychosomatic Medicine*, 1963, **25**, 334-343.

DeCharms, R., & Moeller, G. Values expressed in American children's readers: 1800-1950. *Journal of Abnormal and Social Psychology*, 1962, **64**, 136-142.

Deci, E.L. Effects of externally mediated rewards on intrinsic motivation. *Journal of Personality and Social Psychology*, 1971, **18**, 105-115.

Dodwell, P.C., & Genreau, L. Figural after-effects, sensory coding, expectation and experience. *British Journal of Psychology*, 1969, **60**, 149-167.

Doob, A.N., Carlsmith, J.M., Freedman, J.L., Landauer, T.K., & Tom, S., Jr. Effect of initial selling price on subsequent sales. *Journal of Personality and Social Psychology*, 1969, **2**, 345-350.

Doob, A.N., & Gross, A.E. Status of frustrator as an inhibitor of horn-honking responses. *Journal of Social Psychology*, 1968, **76**, 213-218.

Dornbusch, S., & Hickman, L. Other-directedness in consumer goods advertising: A test of Riesman's historical theory. *Social Forces*, 1959, **38**, 99-102.

Duncan, C.P. Visual figural after-effects as a function of stimulation interval and decay time. *Perceptual and Motor Skills*, 1958, **8**, 203-206.

Duncan, S., & Rosenthal, R. Vocal emphasis in experimenters' instructions as unintended determinant of subjects' responses. *Language and Speech*, 1968 II, Part I, 20-26.

Ebbinghaus, H. *Memory: A contribution to experimental psychology*. (1885) Translated by H.A. Ruger & C.E. Bussenius. New York: Columbia University, 1913.

Edwards, A.L. *The social desirability variable in personality assessment and research*. New York: Dryden, 1957.

Eibl-Eibesfeldt, I. *Ethology: The biology of behavior*. New York: Holt, Rinehart & Winston, 1970.

Eisenman, R., & Huber, H. Creativity, insolence, and attractiveness of female experimenters. *Perceptual and Motor Skills*, 1970, **30**, 515-520.

Ellson, D.G., Davis, R.C., Saltzman, I.J., & Burke, C.J. A report on research on detection of deception. (Contract N6onr-18011 with Office of Naval Research) Bloomington, Indiana: Dept. of Psychology, Indiana University, 1952.

Evans, R.I., & Rozelle, R.M. (Eds.) *Social psychology in life*. Boston: Allyn & Bacon, 1970.

Eysenck, H.J. *Dimensions of personality*. London: Routledge & Kegan Paul, 1947.

Fawl, C.L. *Disturbances experienced by children in their natural habitats*. In R.G. Barker (Ed.), *The stream of behavior*. New York: Appleton-Century-Crofts, 1963, pp. 99-126.

Fellner, C.H. & Marshall, J.R. Kidney donors. In J. McCauley & L. Berkowitz (Eds.), *Altruism and helping behavior*. New York: Academic Press, 1970, pp. 269-281.

Fernberger, S.W. The effect of the attitude of the subject upon the measure of sensitivity. *American Journal of Psychology*, 1914, **25**, 538-543.

Festinger, L. *A theory of cognitive dissonance.* Evanston, Ill.: Row, Peterson, 1957.

Festinger, L., Behavioral support for opinion change. *Public Opinion Quarterly*, 1964, **28**, 404-417.

Festinger, L., & Maccoby, M. On resistance to persuasive communications. *Journal of Abnormal and Social Psychology*, 1964, **68**, 359-368.

Festinger, L., Rieken, H., & Schacter, S. *When prophecy fails.* Minneapolis: University of Minnesota Press, 1956.

Festinger, L., & Thibaut, J. Interpersonal communication in small groups. *Journal of Abnormal and Social Psychology*, 1951, **46**, 92-99.

Fine, R. On the nature of scientific method in psychology. *Psychological Reports*, 1969, **24**, 519-540.

Fisher, S. The role of expectancy in the performance of posthypnotic behavior. *Journal of Abnormal and Social Psychology*, 1954, **49**, 503-507.

Freedman, J.L. Role playing: Psychology by consensus. *Journal of Personality and Social Psychology*, 1969, **13**, 107-114.

Freedman, J.L., & Sears, D.O. Warning, distraction, and resistance to influence. *Journal of Personality and Social Psychology*, 1965, **1**, 262-266.

Friedman, N. *The social nature of psychological research: The psychological experiment as a social interaction.* New York: Basic Books, 1967.

Gaertner, S., & Bickman, L. A non-reactive indicator measure of racial discrimination: The wrong-number technique. In L. Bickman & T. Henchy (Eds.), *Beyond the laboratory: Field research in social psychology.* New York: McGraw-Hill, 1972.

Geer, J.H., & Silverman, I. Treatment of a recurrent nightmare by behavior modification procedures. *Journal of Abnormal Psychology*, 1967, **72**, 188-190.

Gibson, J.J. Adaptation, after-effect, and contrast in the perception of curved lines. *Journal of Experimental Psychology*, 1933, **16**, 1-31.

Goldberg, P.A. Expectancy, choice, and the other person. *Journal of Personality and Social Psychology*, 1965, **2**, 685-691.

Golding, S.L., & Lichtenstein, E. Confession of awareness and prior knowledge of deception as a function of interview set and approval motivation. *Journal of Personality and Social Psychology*, 1970, **14**, 213-223.

Goldman, R., Jaffa, M., & Schacter, S. Yom Kippur, Air France, dormitory food, and the eating behavior of obese and normal persons. *Journal of Personality and Social Psychology*, 1968, **10**, 117-123.

Goldstein, A.P. *Therapist-patient expectancies in psychotherapy.* Elmsford, New York: Pergamon Press, 1962.

Gough, H.G., & Heilbrun, A.B., Jr., *The Adjective Check List manual.* Palo Alto, Calif.: Consulting Psychologists Press, 1965.

Green, D.R. Volunteering and the recall of interrupted tasks. *Journal of Abnormal and Social Psychology*, 1963, **66**, 397-401.

Greenberg, M.S. Role playing: An alternative to deception? *Journal of Personality and Social Psychology*, 1967, **7**, 152-157.

Greenspoon, J. The reinforcing effect of two spoken sounds on the frequency of two responses. *American Journal of Psychology*, 1955, **68**, 409-416.

Gustav, A. Students' attitudes toward compulsory participation in experiments. *Journal of Psychology*, 1962, **53**, 119-125.

Harper, R.S. Perceptual modification of colored figures. *American Journal of Psychology*, 1953, **66**, 86-89.

Hendrick, C., Wallace, B., & Tappenbeck, J. Effect of cognitive set on color perception. *Journal of Personality and Social Psychology*, 1968, **4**, 487-494.

Hess, E.H. Attitude and pupil size. *Scientific American*, 1965, **212**, 46-54.

Hess, E.H., & Polt, J.M. Pupil size as related to interest value of visual stimuli. *Science*, 1960, **132**, 349-350.

Hess, E.H., & Polt, J.M. Changes in pupil size as a measure of taste difference. *Perceptual and Motor Skills*, 1966, **23**, 451-455.

Hess, E.H., Seltzer, A.L., & Shlien, J.M. Pupil response of hetero- and homosexual males to pictures of men and women: A pilot study. *Journal of Abnormal Psychology*, 1965, **70**, 165-168.

Hetherington, M., & Ross, L.E. Effect of sex of subjects, sex of experimenter, and reinforcement condition on serial verbal learning. *Journal of Experimental Psychology*, 1963, **65**, 572-575.

Hoffman, L.R., & Maier, N.R.F. Sex differences, sex composition, and group problem solving. *Journal of Abnormal and Social Psychology*, 1961, **63**, 453-456.

Hoffman, L.R., & Maier, N.R.F. Social factors influencing problem solving in women. *Journal of Personality and Social Psychology*, 1966, 4, 382-390.

Holmes, D. Amount of experience in experiments as a determinant of performance in later experiments. *Journal of Personality and Social Psychology*, 1967, 7, 403-407.

Hornstien, H.A., Masor, H.N., Sole, K., & Heilman, M. Effects of sentiment and completion of a helping act on observer helping: The case for socially mediated Zeigarnik effects. *Journal of Personality and Social Psychology*, 1971, 17, 107-112.

Horowitz, I.A. Effects of volunteering, fear arousal, and number of communications on attitude change. *Journal of Personality and Social Psychology*, 1969, 11, 34-37.

Horowitz, I.A., & Gumenik, W.E. Effects of the volunteer subject, choice, and fear arousal on attitude change. *Journal of Experimental Social Psychology*, 1970, 6, 293-303.

Horst, L. Research in the effect of the experimenter's expectancies—A laboratory model of social influence. Unpublished manuscript, Harvard University, 1966.

Hovland, C.I. Reconciling conflicting results derived from experimental and survey studies of attitude change. *American Psychologist*, 1959, 14, 8-17.

Hovland, C.I., & Sears, R. Minor studies in aggression: VI. Correlation of lynchings with economic indices. *Journal of Psychology*, 1940, 9, 301-310.

Hovland, C.I., & Weiss, W. The influence of source credibility on communication effectiveness. *Public Opinion Quarterly*, 1951, 15, 635-650.

Hurwitz, S., & Jenkins, V. The effects of experimenter expectancy on performance of simple learning tasks. Unpublished manuscript, Harvard University, 1966.

Insko, C.A. Verbal reinforcement of attitude. *Journal of Personality and Social Psychology*, 1965, 2, 621-623.

Insko, C.A., & Butzine, K.W. Rapport, awareness, and verbal reinforcement of attitude. *Journal of Personality and Social Psychology*, 1967, 6, 225-228.

Insko, C.A., & Cialdini, R.B. A test of three interpretations of attitudinal verbal reinforcement. *Journal of Personality and Social Psychology*, 1969, 12, 333-341.

Insko, C.A., & Oakes, W.F. Awareness and the "conditioning" of attitudes. *Journal of Personality and Social Psychology*, 1966, 4, 487-496.

Janis, I.L., & Feshbach, S. Effects of fear-arousing communications. *Journal of Abnormal and Social Psychology*, 1953, **48**, 78-92.

Janis, I.L., & Field, P.B. Sex differences and personality factors related to personality. In C.I. Hovland & I.L. Janis (Eds.), *Personality and persuasibility*. New Haven: Yale University Press, 1959, pp. 55-68.

Janis, I.L., Kaye, D., & Kirschner, P. Facilitating effects of "eating-while-reading" on responsiveness to persuasive communications. *Journal of Personality and Social Psychology*, 1965, **1**, 181-185.

Johnson, R.W. Subject performance as affected by experimenter expectancy, sex of experimenter, and verbal reinforcement. Unpublished master's thesis, University of New Brunswick, 1967.

Johnson, H.H., Tovcivia, J.M., & Poprick, M.A. Effects of source credibility on the relationship between authoritarianism and attitude change. *Journal of Personality and Social Psychology*, 1968, **9**, 179-183.

Jourard, S.M. *Disclosing man to himself*. Princeton, N.J.: D. Van Nostrand, 1968.

Jourard, S.M. The effects of experimenter's self-disclosure on subjects' behavior. In C.D. Spielberger (Ed.), *Current topics in clinical and community psychology*. New York: Academic Press, 1969, pp. 109-150.

Joy, V.L. Repression-sensitization and interpersonal behavior. Paper read at American Psychological Association, Philadelphia, August 1963.

Jung, J. Current practices and problems in the use of college students for psychological research. *Canadian Psychologist*, 1969, **10**, 280-290.

Katz, D., Sarnoff, I., & McClintock, C.G. Ego defense and attitude change. *Human Relations*, 1956, **9**, 27-46.

Kelman, H.C. Human use of human subjects: The problem of deception in social psychological experiments. *Psychological Bulletin*, 1967, **67**, 1-11.

Kelman, H.C. The rights of the subject in social research: An analysis in terms of relative power and legitimacy. *American Psychologist*, 1972, **27**, 989-1016.

Kinsey, A.C., Pomeroy, W.B., & Martin, C.E. *Sexual behavior in the human male*. Philadelphia: W.B. Saunders, 1948.

Klinger, E. Modeling effects on achievement imagery. *Journal of Personality and Social Psychology*, 1967, **1**, 49-62.

Knox, R.E., & Inkster, J.A. Postdecision dissonance at post time.

Journal of Personality and Social Psychology, 1968, **8**, 319-323.

Koch, S. Psychology cannot be a coherent science. *Psychology Today*, 1969, **3**, **14**, 64-68.

Kohler, W., & Wallach, H. Figural after-effects: An investigation of visual processes. *Proceedings of the American Philosophical Society*, 1944, **88**, 269-357.

Krasner, L. Studies of the conditioning of verbal behavior. *Psychological Bulletin*, 1958, **55**, 148-171.

Kruglanski, A.W. Much ado about the "volunteer artifacts." *Journal of Personality and Social Psychology*, 1973, **28**, 348-354.

Lana, R.E. Three theoretical interpretations of order effects in persuasive communications. *Psychological Bulletin*, 1964, **61**, 314-320.

Lana, R.E. Pretest sensitization. In R. Rosenthal & R.L. Rosnow (Eds.), *Artifact in behavioral research.* New York: Academic Press, 1969, pp. 121-146.

Lang, P.J. Experimental studies of desensitization psychotherapy. In Wolpe, J., Salter, A., & Reyna, L.J., *The conditioning therapies.* New York: Holt, Rinehart & Winston, 1964.

Lang, P.J., Lazovik, A.D., & Reynolds, D.J. Desensitization, suggestibility and pseudotherapy. *Journal of Abnormal and Social Psychology*, 1965, **70**, 395-402.

Larsen, K.S. Authoritarianism, hawkishness and attitude change as related to high and low status communication. *Perceptual and Motor Skills*, 1969, **28**, 114.

Lashley, K.S., Chow, K.L., & Semmes, J. An examination of the electrical field theory of cerebral integration. *Psychological Review*, 1951, **58**, 123-136.

Latané, B. Field studies on altruistic compliance. *Representative Research in Social Psychology*, 1970, **1**, 49-60.

Lazarus, R.S., & Alfert, E. Short circuiting of threat by experimentally altering cognitive appraisal. *Journal of Abnormal and Social Psychology*, 1964, **69**, 195-205.

Lefcourt, H.M. Repression-sensitization: A measure of the evaluation of emotional expression. *Journal of Consulting Psychology*, 1966, **30**, 444-449.

Leventhal, H., & Niles, P. A field experiment on fear arousal with data on the validity of questionnaire measures. *Journal of Personality*, 1964, **32**, 459-479.

Levin, S.M. The effect of awareness on verbal conditioning. *Journal of Experimental Psychology*, 1961, **61**, 67-75.

Levy, L.H. Awareness, learning and the beneficent subject as expert witness. *Journal of Personality and Social Psychology*, 1967, **6**, 365-370.

Linde, T.F., & Patterson, C.H. Influence of orthopedic disability on conformity behavior. *Journal of Abnormal and Social Psychology*, 1964, **68**, 115-118.

Lindgren, H.C., & Byrne, D. *Psychology: An introduction to a behavioral science.* New York: Wiley, 1971.

Lipset, S.M., Trow, M., & Coleman, J. *Union democracy.* New York: Free Press, 1956.

Littig, L.W., & Waddell, C.M. Sex and experimenter interaction in serial learning. *Journal of Verbal Learning and Verbal Behavior*, 1967, **6**, 676-678.

Livant, W.P. A comparison of noun and verb forms on the semantic differential. *Journal of Verbal Learning and Verbal Behavior*, 1963, **1**, 357-360.

Locke, H.J. Are volunteer interviewees representative? *Social Problems*, 1954, **1**, 143-146.

Lomont, J.F. The repression-sensitization dimension in relation to anxiety responses. *Journal of Consulting Psychology*, 1965, **29**, 84-86.

Maier, N.R.F. An aspect of human reasoning. *British Journal of Psychology*, 1933, **24**, 144-155.

Manis, M., & Ruppe, J. The carryover phenomenon: The persistence of reinforced behavior despite the absence of a conscious behavioral intention. *Journal of Personality and Social Psychology*, 1969, **11**, 397-407.

Mann, L., & Taylor, K.F. Queue counting: The effect of motives upon estimates of numbers in waiting lines. *Journal of Personality and Social Psychology*, 1969, **12**, 95-103.

Marcia, J.E., Rubin, B.M., & Efran, J.S. Systematic desensitization: Expectancy change or counterconditioning? *Journal of Abnormal Psychology*, 1969, **74**, 382-387.

Marwit, S.J. Communication of tester bias by means of modeling. *Journal of Projective Techniques and Personality Assessment*, 1969, **33**, 345-352.

Marwit, S.J., & Marcia, J.E. Tester bias and response to projective instruments. *Journal of Consulting Psychology*, 1967, **31**, 253-258.

Masling, J. Role-related behavior of the subject and psychologist and its effects upon psychological data. In D.L. Levine (Ed.),

Nebraska symposium on motivation. Lincoln: University of Nebraska Press, 1966, pp. 67-103.

Maslow, A.H. & Sakoda, J.M. Volunteer-error in the Kinsey study. *Journal of Abnormal and Social Psychology,* 1952, **47**, 259-262.

McClelland, D.C., Atkinson, J.W., Clark, R.A., & Lowell, E.L. *The achievement motive.* New York: Appleton-Century-Crofts, 1953.

McClintock, C.G. Personality syndromes and attitude change. *Journal of Personality,* 1958, **26**, 479-493.

McGuire, W.J. Personality and susceptibility to social influence. In E.F. Borgatta & W.W. Lambert, *Handbook of personality theory and research.* New York: Rand McNally, 1966, pp. 1130-1188.

McNemar, Q. Opinion attitude methodology. *Psychological Bulletin,* 1946, **43**, 289-374.

McQuigan, F.J. The experimenter. A neglected stimulus object. *Psychological Bulletin,* 1963, **60**, 421-428.

Menges, R.J. Openness and honesty versus coercion and deception in psychological research. *American Psychologist,* 1973, **28**, 1030-1034.

Middlebrook, P.N. *Social psychology and modern life.* New York: Knopf, 1974.

Milgram, S. Behavioral study of obedience. *Journal of Abnormal and Social Psychology,* 1963, **67**, 371-378.

Milgram, S. Issues in the study of obedience: A reply to Baumrind. *American Psychologist,* 1964, **19**, 848-852.

Miller, A.G. (Ed.) *The social psychology of psychological research.* New York: Free Press, 1972.

Minor, M.W. Experimenter-expectancy effect as a function of evaluation apprehension. *Journal of Personality and Social Psychology,* 1970, **15**, 326-332.

Morris, D. Must we have zoos? *Life,* November 8, 1968, pp. 78-86.

Morse, S., & Gergen, K.J. Social comparison, self-consistency, and the concept of self. *Journal of Personality and Social Psychology,* 1970, **16**, 148-156.

Newberry, B.J. Truth telling in subjects with information about experiments: Who is being deceived? *Journal of Personality and Social Psychology,* 1973, **25**, 369-374.

Newcomb, T.M. *The acquaintance process.* New York: Holt, 1961.

Nunnally, J.C., Knott, P.D., Duchnowski, A., & Parker, R. Pupillary response as a general measure of activation. *Perception and Psychophysics,* 1967, **2**, 149-155.

Oakes, W.F. Verbal operant conditioning, intertrial activity, awareness, and the extended interview. *Journal of Personality and Social Psychology*, 1967, **6**, 198-202.

Oakes, W.F. External validity and the use of real people as subjects. *American Psychologist*, 1972, **27**, 959-962.

Olmstead, J.A., & Blake, R.R. The use of simulated groups to produce modifications in judgment. *Journal of Personality*, 1955, **23**, 335-345.

Orne, M.T. The nature of hypnosis: Artifact and essence. *Journal of Abnormal and Social Psychology*, 1959, **58**, 277-299.

Orne, M.T. On the social psychology of the psychological experiment: With particular reference to demand characteristics and their implications. *American Psychologist*, 1962, **17**, 776-783.

Orne, M.T. Demand characteristics and their implications for real life: The importance of quasi-controls. Presented at the symposium titled "Ethical and methodological problems in social psychological research." American Psychological Association, Chicago, Illinois, September, 1965.

Orne, M.T. Demand characteristics and the concept of quasi-controls. In R. Rosenthal & R.L. Rosnow (Eds.), *Artifact in behavioral research*. New York: Academic Press, 1969, pp. 143-179.

Orne, M.T., & Evans, F.J. Social control in the psychological experiment: Antisocial behavior and hypnosis. *Journal of Personality and Social Psychology*, 1965, **1**, 189-200.

Orne, M.T., & Evans, F.J. Inadvertent termination of hypnosis with hypnotized and simulating subjects. *International Journal of Clinical and Experimental Hypnosis*, 1966, **14**, 61-78.

Orne, M.T., & Scheibe, K.E. The contribution of non-deprivation factors in the production of sensory deprivation effects: The psychology of the "panic button." *Journal of Abnormal and Social Psychology*, 1964, **68**, 3-12.

Orne, M.T., Sheehan, P.W., & Evans, F.J. Occurrence of posthypnotic behavior outside the experimental setting. *Journal of Personality and Social Psychology*, 1968, **9**, 189-196.

Osgood, C.E., Suci, G.J., & Tannenbaum, P.H. *The measurement of meaning*. Urbana: University of Illinois, 1957.

Osgood, C.E., & Walker, E. Motivation and language behavior: A content analysis of suicide notes. *Journal of Abnormal and Social Psychology*, 1959, **59**, 58-67.

Page, M.M. Social psychology of a classical conditioning of attitudes experiment. *Journal of Personality and Social Psychology*, 1969, **11**, 177-186.

Page, M.M. Demand awareness, subject sophistication, and the effectiveness of a verbal "reinforcement." *Journal of Personality*, 1970, **38**, 287-301.

Page, M.M. Effects of evaluation apprehension on cooperation in verbal conditioning. *Journal of Experimental Research in Personality*, 1971, **5**, 85-91.

Page, M.M., & Scheidt, R.H. The elusive weapons effect: Demand awareness, evaluation apprehension, and slightly sophisticated subjects. *Journal of Personality and Social Psychology*, 1971, **20**, 304-318.

Page, S. Social interaction and experimenter effects in the verbal conditioning experiment. *Canadian Journal of Psychology*, 1971, **25**, 463-475.

Page, S. The social psychology of research: Attitudes and practices of psychologists. *Canadian Journal of Behavioral Science*, 1975 (in press).

Peabody, D. Attitude content and agreement set in scales of authoritarianism, dogmatism, anti-Semitism, and economic conservatism. *Journal of Abnormal and Social Psychology*, 1961, **63**, 1-11.

Peabody, D. Authoritarianism scales and response bias. *Psychological Bulletin*, 1966, **65**, 11-23.

Planck, M. *The universe in the light of modern physics.* London: George Allen & Unwin, 1937.

Rickard, H.C., Dignam, P.J., & Horner, R.F. Verbal manipulations in a psychotherapeutic relationship. *Journal of Clinical Psychology*, 1960, **16**, 364-367.

Riecken, H. A program for research on experiments in social psychology. In N.F. Washburne (Ed.), *Decisions, values and groups.* Vol. II. Elmsford, N.Y.: Pergamon Press, 1962, 25-41.

Ring, K. Experimental social psychology: Some sober questions about frivolous values. *Journal of Experimental Social Psychology*, 1967, **3**, 113-123.

Rogers, J.M. Operant conditioning in a quasi-therapeutic setting. *Journal of Abnormal and Social Psychology*, 1960, **60**, 247-252.

Rokeach, M. The double agreement phenomenon: Three hypotheses. *Psychological Review*, 1963, **70**, 304-309.

Rosenberg, M.J. Cognitive reorganization in response to the hypnotic reversal of attitudinal affect. *Journal of Personality*, 1960, **28**, 39-63. (a)

Rosenberg, M.J. A structural theory of attitude dynamics. *Public*

Opinion Quarterly, 1960, **24**, 319-340. (b)

Rosenberg, M.J. When dissonance fails: On eliminating evaluation apprehension from attitude measurement. *Journal of Personality and Social Psychology*, 1965, **1**, 28-42.

Rosenberg, M.J. The conditions and consequences of evaluation apprehension. In R. Rosenthal & R. Rosnow (Eds.), *Artifact in behavioral research*. New York: Academic Press, 1969, pp. 280-349.

Rosenfeld, H., & Baer, D.M. Unnoticed verbal conditioning of an aware experimenter by a more aware subject: The double-agent effect. *Psychological Review*, 1969, **76**, 425-432.

Rosenthal, R. An attempt at the experimental induction of the defense mechanism of projection. Unpublished doctoral dissertation, U.C.L.A., 1956.

Rosenthal, R. On the social psychology of the psychological experiment: The experimenter's hypothesis as unintended determinant of experimental results. *American Scientist*, 1963, **51**, 268-283.

Rosenthal, R. The volunteer subject. *Human Relations*, 1965, **18**, 389-406.

Rosenthal, R. *Experimenter effects in behavioral research*. New York: Appleton-Century-Crofts, 1966.

Rosenthal, R. Interpersonal expectations: Effects of the experimenter's hypothesis. In R. Rosenthal & R.L. Rosnow (Eds.), *Artifact in behavioral research*. New York: Academic Press, 1969, pp. 181-277.

Rosenthal, R., & Fode, K.L. The effect of experimenter bias on the performance of the albino rat. *Behavioral Science*, 1963, **8**, 183-189.

Rosenthal, R., & Jacobson, L. *Pygmalion in the classroom: Teacher expectation and pupils' intellectual development*. New York: Holt, Rinehart & Winston, 1968.

Rosenthal, R., & Lawson, R. A longitudinal study of the effects of experimenter bias on the operant learning of laboratory rats. *Journal of Psychiatric Research*, 1964, **2**, 61-72.

Rosenthal, R., Persinger, G.W., Vikan-Kline, L., & Fode, K.L. The effects of early data returns on data subsequently obtained by outcome-biased experimenters. *Sociometry*, 1963, **26**, 487-498.

Rosenthal, R., & Rosnow, R.L. The volunteer subject. In R. Rosenthal & R.L. Rosnow (Eds.), *Artifact in behavioral research*. New York: Academic Press, 1969, pp. 59-118.

Rosenzweig, S. The experimental situation as a psychological problem. *Psychological Review*, 1933, **40**, 337-354.

Rosenzweig, S. A suggestion for making verbal personality tests more valid. *Psychological Review*, 1934, **41**, 400-401.

Rosnow, R.L. One sided versus two sided communication under indirect awareness of persuasive intent. *Public Opinion Quarterly*, 1968, pp. 95-101.

Rosnow, R., & Rosenthal, R. Volunteer subjects and the results of opinion change studies. *Psychological Reports*, 1966, **19**, 1183-1187.

Rosnow, R.L., & Rosenthal, R. Volunteer effects in behavioral research. In K.H. Craik, B. Kleinmuntz, R.L. Rosnow, R. Rosenthal, J.A. Cheyne, & R.H. Walters, *New directions in psychology*, Vol. IV. New York: Holt, Rinehart & Winston, 1970.

Rosnow, R.L., & Suls, J. Reactive effects of pretesting in attitude research. *Journal of Personality and Social Psychology*, 1970, **15**, 338-343.

Rotter, J.B., & Rafferty, J.E. *Manual for the Rotter Incomplete Sentences Blank: College form.* New York: Psychological Corporation, 1950.

Rowland, L.W. Will hypnotized persons try to harm themselves or others? *Journal of Abnormal and Social Psychology*, 1939, **34**, 114-117.

Samelson, F. Agreement set and anticontent attitudes in the F scales: A reinterpretation. *Journal of Abnormal and Social Psychology*, 1964, **68**, 338-342.

Sarason, I.G. Interrelationships among individual difference variables, behavior in psychotherapy and verbal conditioning. *Journal of Abnormal and Social Psychology*, 1958, **56**, 339-344.

Schulman, G.I. Asch conformity studies: Conformity to the experimenter and/or to the group? *Sociometry*, 1967, **30**, 26-40.

Schacter, S. *The psychology of affiliation: Experimental studies of the sources of gregariousness.* Stanford: Stanford University Press, 1959.

Schultz, D.P. The human subject in psychological research. *Psychological Bulletin*, 1969, **72**, 214-228.

Scott, T.R. Social reinforcement of aggressive sentences. Unpublished Ph.D. Dissertation, University of Nebraska, 1958.

Sechrest, L., & Olson, K.L. Graffiti in four types of institutions of higher learning. Unpublished paper, Northwestern University, 1966.

Secord, P.F., & Backman, C.W. *Social psychology.* New York: McGraw-Hill, 1964.

Seeman, J. Deception in psychological research. *American Psychologist*, 1969, **24**, 1025-1028.

Sheehan, P.W. E-expectancy and the role of awareness in verbal conditioning. *Psychological Reports*, 1969, **24**, 203-206.

Sherif, M., & Sherif, C.W. *Reference groups: Explorations into the conformity and deviation of adolescents.* New York: Harper & Row, 1964.

Sherman, S.R. Demand characteristics in an experiment on attitude change. *Sociometry*, 1967, **30**, 246-260.

Shor, R.E. Physiological effects of painful stimulation during hypnotic analgesia under conditions designed to minimize anxiety. *International Journal of Clinical and Experimental Hypnosis*, 1962, **10**, 183-202.

Shulman, A.D., & Silverman, I. Profile of social psychology: A preliminary application of "reference analysis." *Journal of the History of the Behavioral Sciences*, 1972, **8**, 232-236.

Shulman, A.D., & Silverman, I. Social desirability and need approval: Some paradoxical data and a conceptual reevaluation. *British Journal of Social and Clinical Psychology*, 1974, **13**, 27-32.

Shultz, T.R., & Hartup, W.H. Performance under social reinforcement as a function of masculinity-feminity of experimenter and subject. *Journal of Personality and Social Psychology*, 1967, **6**, 337-341.

Sigall, H., Aronson, E., & Van Hoose, T. The cooperative subject: Myth or reality? *Journal of Experimental Social Psychology*, 1970, **6**, 1-10.

Silverman, I. Motives underlying the behavior of the subject in the psychological experiment. Presented at the Symposium titled "Ethical and methodological problems in social psychological research." American Psychological Association, Chicago, Illinois, September, 1965.

Silverman, I. Role-related behavior of subjects in laboratory studies of attitude change. *Journal of Personality and Social Psychology*, 1968, **8**, 343-348. (a)

Silverman, I. Expectancy disconfirmation and the choice of negative alternatives: Dissonance avoidance or situational demands? In R.P. Abelson, E. Aronson, W.J. McGuire, T.M. Newcomb, M.J. Rosenberg, & P.H. Tannenbaum, (Eds.), *Theories of cognitive consistency: A sourcebook.* New York: Rand McNally, 1968. (b)

Silverman, I. The effects of experimenter outcome expectancy on latency of word association. *Journal of Clinical Psychology*, 1968, **24**, 60-63. (c)

Silverman, I. Crisis in social psychology: The relevance of relevance. *American Psychologist*, 1971, **26**, 583-584.

Silverman, I. The experimenter: A (still) neglected stimulus object. *Canadian Psychologist*, 1974, **15**, 258-270.

Silverman, I., Ford, L.H., & Morganti, J.B. Inter-related effects of social desirability, sex, self-esteem and complexity of argument on persuasibility. *Journal of Personality*, 1966, **34**, 555-568.

Silverman, I., & Geer, J.H. The elimination of a recurrent nightmare by desensitization of a related phobia. *Behavior Research and Therapy*, 1968, **6**, 109-111.

Silverman, I., & Kleinman, D. A response deviance interpretation of the effects of experimentally induced frustration on prejudice. *Journal of Experimental Research in Personality*, 1967, **2**, 150-153.

Silverman, I., & Margulis, S. Experiment title as a source of sampling bias in commonly used "subject-pool" procedures. *Canadian Psychologist*, 1973, **14**, 197-201.

Silverman, I., & Regula, C.R. Evaluation apprehension, demand characteristics, and the effects of distraction on persuasibility. *Journal of Social Psychology*, 1968, **75**, 273-281.

Silverman, I., & Shulman, A.D. Effects of hunger on responses to demand characteristics in the measurement of persuasion. *Psychonomic Science*, 1969, **15**, 201-202.

Silverman, I., & Shulman, A.D. A conceptual model of artifact in attitude change studies. *Sociometry*, 1970, **33**, 97-107.

Silverman, I., Shulman, A.D., & Wiesenthal, D. Effects of deceiving and debriefing psychological subjects on performance in later experiments. *Journal of Personality and Social Psychology*, 1970, **14**, 203-212.

Silverman, I., Shulman, A.D., & Wiesenthal, D.L. The experimenter as a source of variance in psychological research: Modeling and sex effects. *Journal of Personality and Social Psychology*, 1972, **21**, 219-227.

Smart, R. Subject selection bias in psychological research. *Canadian Psychologist*, 1966, **7a**, 115-121.

Snadowsky, A. (Ed.). *Social psychology research: Laboratory-field relationships.* New York: Free Press, 1972.

Sommer, R. *Personal space: The behavioral basis of design.* Englewood Cliffs: Prentice-Hall, 1969.

Spielberger, C.D., & Levin, S.M. What is learned in verbal conditioning? *Journal of Verbal Learning and Verbal Behavior*, 1962, **1**, 125-132.

Spielberger, C.D., Levin, S.M., & Shepard, M. The effects of awareness and attitude toward reinforcement on the operant conditioning of verbal behavior. *Journal of Personality*, 1962, **30**, 106-121.

Staats, A. Experimental demand characteristics and the classical conditioning of attitudes. *Journal of Personality and Social Psychology*, 1969, **11**, 187-192.

Staats, A.W., & Staats, C.K. Attitudes established by classical conditioning. *Journal of Abnormal and Social Psychology*, 1958, **57**, 37-40.

Staats, C.K., & Staats, A.W. Meaning established by classical conditioning. *Journal of Experimental Psychology*, 1957, **54**, 74-80.

Stricker, G. Scapegoating: An experimental investigation. *Journal of Abnormal and Social Psychology*, 1963, **67**, 125-131.

Stricker, L. The true deceiver. *Psychological Bulletin*, 1967, **68**, 13-20.

Stricker, L.J., Messick, S., & Jackson, D.N. Suspicion of deception: Implications for conformity research. *Journal of Personality and Social Psychology*, 1967, **5**, 379-389.

Stumberg, D. A comparison of sophisticated and naive subjects by the association-reaction method. *American Journal of Psychology*, 1925, **36**, 88-95.

Sutcliffe, J.P. "Credulous" and "skeptical" views of hypnotic phenomena: Experiments on esthesia, hallucination, and delusion. *Journal of Abnormal and Social Psychology*, 1961, **62**, 189-200.

Taffel, C. Anxiety and the conditioning of verbal behavior. *Journal of Abnormal and Social Psychology*, 1955, **51**, 496-501.

Timmons, E.O. Experiments in conditioning operant verbal behavior. Unpublished Ph.D. Dissertation, University of Tennessee, 1959.

Tinbergen, N. Ethology and stress disease. *Science*, 1974, **184**, 20-27.

Tinklepaugh, O.L. An experimental study of representational factors in monkeys. *Journal of Comparative and Physiological Psychology*, 1928, **8**, 197-236.

Titchener, E.B. Simple reactions. *Mind*, 1895, 4, 74-81.

Titchener, E.B. *Experimental psychology*. New York: Macmillan, 1901.

Titchener, E.B. Prolegomena to a study of introspection. *American Journal of Psychology*, 1912, **23**, 447-448.

Ullman, L.P., Krasner, L., & Collins, B.J. Modification of behavior through verbal conditioning. *Journal of Abnormal and Social Psychology*, 1961, **62**, 128-132.

Ullman, L.P., & McReynolds, P. Differential perceptual recognition in psychiatric patients: Empirical findings and theoretical formulation. Paper read at American Psychological Association, Philadelphia, August 1963.

Valins, S. Cognitive effects of false heart-rate feedback. *Journal of Personality and Social Psychology*, 1966, 4, 400-408.

Vaughan, G.M. The trans-situational aspect of conforming behavior. *Journal of Personality*, 1964, 32, 335-354.

Verbruggen, F. Looking for Leon Festinger in the 18th century. Unpublished paper, University of Ghent, 1973.

Vinacke, W.E. Deceiving experimental subjects. *American Psychologist*, 1954, 9, 155.

Walster, E., Berscheid, E., Abrahams, D., & Aronson, V. Effectiveness of debriefing following deception experiments. *Journal of Personality and Social Psychology*, 1967, 6, 371-380.

Ware, J.R., Kowal, B., & Baker, R.A., Jr. The role of experimenter attitude and contingent reinforcement in a vigilance task. Technical report. Human Research Unit, Fort Knox, Kentucky, 1963.

Webb, E.J., Campbell, D.T., Schwartz, R.D., & Sechrest, L. *Unobtrusive measures: Nonreactive research in the social sciences.* Chicago: Rand McNally, 1966.

Wechsler, D. *The measurement and appraisal of adult intelligence.* Baltimore: Williams and Wilkins, 1958.

Weiss, R.L., Ullman, L.P., & Krasner, L. On the relationship between hypnotizability and response to verbal operant conditioning. *Psychological Reports*, 1960, 6, 415-426.

Weitz, J., & Post, A. A stereoscopic study of figural after-effects. *American Journal of Psychology*, 1948, 61, 59-61.

Wells, E.F. The effect of attitude on feeling. *American Journal of Psychology*, 1930, 42, 573-580.

White, H.A., & Shumsky, D.A. Prior information and "awareness" in verbal conditioning. *Journal of Personality and Social Psychology*, 1972, 24, 162-165.

White, R.W. A preface to the theory of hypnotism. *Journal of Abnormal and Social Psychology*, 1941, 36, 477-505.

Wightman, W.P.D. *The growth of scientific ideas.* New Haven: Yale University Press, 1953.

Willems, E.P. Planning a rationale for naturalistic research. In E.P. Willems and H.L. Raush (Eds.), *Naturalistic viewpoints in psychological research.* New York: Holt, Rinehart & Winston, 1969, pp. 44-71.

Willis, R.H., & Willis, Y.A. Role playing versus deception: An experimental comparison. *Journal of Personality and Social Psychology*, 1970, **16**, 472-477.

Winkel, G.H., & Sarason, I.G. Subject, experimenter and situational variables in research on anxiety. *Journal of Abnormal and Social Psychology*, 1964, **68**, 601-608.

Wispé, L.G., & Freshley, H.B. Race, sex, and sympathetic helping behavior: The broken bag caper. *Journal of Personality and Social Psychology*, 1971, **17**, 59-65.

Wolpe, J. *Psychotherapy by reciprocal inhibition*. Stanford: Stanford University Press, 1958.

Woodworth, R.S., & Schlossberg, H. *Experimental psychology*. New York: Holt, 1960.

Young, P.C. Antisocial uses of hypnosis. In L.M. LeCron (Ed.), *Experimental hypnosis*. New York: Macmillan, 1952, pp. 376-409.

Zeigarnik, B. Das behalten erledigter und unerledigter handlungen. *Psychologische Forschung*, **9**, 1-85.

Zipple, B., & Norman, R.D. Party switching, authoritarianism, and dogmatism in the 1964 election. *Psychological Reports*, 1966, **19**, 667-670.

Zucker, R.A., Manosevitz, M., & Lanyon, R.I. Birth order, anxiety and affiliation during a crisis. *Journal of Personality and Social Psychology*, 1968, **8**, 354-359.

Author Index

Subject Index